To Claudia and Mark —
My great friends!'s

Mary Scott Roberts

—2012—

PLATFORM

PRESS

BUCKS COUNTY
PENNSYLVANIA

Collaboration
NATION

HOW PUBLIC-PRIVATE VENTURES ARE REVOLUTIONIZING THE BUSINESS OF GOVERNMENT

MARY SCOTT NABERS

Published in the United States by
Platform Press
The nonfiction imprint of
Winans Kuenstler Publishing, LLC
Doylestown, Pennsylvania 18901 USA
www.wkpublishing.com

Platform Press and colophon
are registered trademarks

ISBN: 978-0-9829461-6-9

First Edition

Dedication

*To my political heroes and mentors,
valued business partners,
trusting clients, and
all conscientious public officials.*

It is better for the public to procure at the market whatever the market can supply; because there it is by competition kept up in quality, and reduced to its minimum price.
                                —Thomas Jefferson

Acknowledgments

I have been blessed with great teachers, business partners, political mentors and loyal friends. It would be impossible to produce a list of all the individuals I should thank for their contributions to this book. I will undoubtedly leave out someone who deserves to be listed, but I'll attempt to list (in alphabetical order) some who deserve to be recognized for their contributions.

My business partners have been helpful in every conceivable way. These individuals are true experts and I depend on them every day. There are no words to adequately express the gratitude I feel for them. This book would not have been possible had it not been for the assistance, advice and commitment from these individuals:

Charissa Aguilar, Ben Barnes, J. Lyn Carl, Rich DePalma, Dawn Doyle, David Duncan, Gay Erwin, Cayah Haney, Dave Horton, Tommy Huntress, Jake Jenkins, Casey Kelly, Laura Matisi, Patti Maugham, Scott Moorhead, Reagan Weil, and Kirk Yoshida.

Some of the subject matter experts, readers, researchers, advisors, and government contracting sector experts who provided assistance and inspiration include:

Nora Belcher, Ann Fuelberg Bishop, Kent Capterton, Leah Clark, Tom Davies, John Fleming, Brian Francis, Bill Kuntz, Richard Lewis, Jerry Martin, Jim Ray, Barbara Richey, Karen Robinson, Steve Robinson, Trey Salinas, Ed Serna, Jim Shelgren, Brian Tulga and Leslie Ward.

Then there are my friends and extended family members who lived through the last year and a half with me while the book was being developed. They have been tolerant, encouraging, and patient. Many times they fed me and listened over dinner while I talked much longer than they would have preferred about some part of the book. On a number of occasions, a few expressed doubts that my personality would ever be good again, but overall I have had strong support that made the ordeal bearable. Thanks to:

Janie and Pat Boyle, Carolyn and Nub Donaldson, Gregg Donley, Peggy and Andy Greenawalt, Jill Griffin, Jane Hays, Janice Hartrick, Missy and Ron Jackson, Anita and Earl Maxwell, Paula and Steve Morelock, Merriman Morton, Gayle Pickering and Ed Edmondson, Sharon Schweitzer, John Robinson, Kathy and Randy Taylor, and Kathy and Terry Patrick.

My immediate family has been helpful and supportive and were willing to forgive me for abandoning all kinds of chores I once handled with enthusiasm. Perhaps the most complaints were voiced over my complete abandonment of any and all activities associated with being in a kitchen. Scott, Tim and Karen, thank you for your love and understanding and for taking over lots of additional responsibilities for the past year and a half. You've been wonderful.

Contents

About the Author

Mary Scott Nabers is president and CEO of Strategic Partnerships, Inc. (SPI), a government affairs, business development, procurement consulting, and research company that has helped secure contracts worth billions of dollars for its clients since 1995.

Nabers served a term as a Texas Railroad commissioner during the administration of Governor Ann Richards, overseeing the regulation of the state's $65 billion energy and transportation complexes.

From 1984 to 1992, she served as the commissioner representing business at the Texas Employment Commission, where she founded the Texas Business Council. Commissioner Nabers, who previously owned radio stations and newspapers, also wrote a weekly column for more than one hundred newspapers, hosted a weekly radio program, and published a monthly business publication with a circulation of 160,000.

She has represented Texas on numerous national boards,

earning a reputation for initiating innovative programs in government, and has been active on the professional speaking circuit for twenty years.

At Strategic Partnerships, Inc., she publishes the *Texas Government Insider*, a weekly online publication, and *Government Contracting Pipeline*, a national publication that focuses on upcoming opportunities throughout the United States.

Nabers earned her MBA from University of Texas at Austin.

Author's Note

The goal of this book is to open a window between government and business so each can get a better sense of the issues and challenges facing the other.

The book is organized in such a way that those with a specific interest in one aspect or another can find what most interests them. A full reading will give a 360-degree perspective.

Part One provides an overview, discussion of trends, and examples of projects and situations that illustrate this fast-changing marketplace.

Part Two goes inside the specific area of public-private partnerships, how they work, why they are becoming attractive, and what goes into successful collaborations.

Part Three goes into greater detail about different kinds of contracting, the culture of government, the culture of the private sector, the stakeholders involved in most procurements, and further detail about P3s (public-private partnerships) with examples.

Part Four comprises excerpts from interviews with public officials, subject area experts, and vendors.

Part Five comprises developments around the nation at the state level regarding privatization initiatives and developments. The material is adapted with permission from the 2011 Annual Privatization Report published by the Reason Foundation.

Part Six provides some practical, specific tasks and research that are recommended before a potential government vendor sits down to talk with a public official.

Introduction

By the time I was twelve years old, I was accustomed to serious discussions on current events, politics, and business with both my parents but especially with my father who, in addition to being a newspaper publisher, was the mayor of our small West Texas town. When we sat down to meals, I was expected to have opinions that I could argue effectively. I loved current events and politics and felt sure that someday I would go into government. Along the way, I discovered I had a strong entrepreneurial streak.

At the age of sixteen, I started my first business—a summer day camp that was successful enough to last through three seasons. By the time I got to college, I considered myself a serial entrepreneur.

My high school sweetheart, Lynn Nabers, became my husband shortly after we finished high school. We worked our way through college and law school, and after graduation, he ran for the state legislature. It seemed like a long shot but he won and served for the next fourteen years.

Our family was growing and so was my interest in capitalism. I built a small media company, with two radio stations and a newspaper. During those years as a business owner, my interactions with government were eye-opening and exasperating. It was clear regulators had little to offer in the way of assistance to small firms. The bureaucracy was confusing and at times impenetrable. My media properties gave me a bully pulpit to speak out about injustices I thought the state inflicted on small business.

After I sold the media company, I was offered the opportunity to put my ideas into action when I was appointed by the governor to serve as a commissioner of the Texas Employment Commission, TEC (now the Texas Workforce Commission). My responsibilities included representing the interests of all 380,000 of the state's employers.

The first attempt at communicating with my constituency was an adventure. During my first week I learned that the agency was about to send out a notice announcing an unusually large increase in the unemployment tax. I knew from firsthand experience that this news would be greeted with outrage and complaints.

As a communications expert, I came up with an idea that was innovative and I thought might be effective. I wrote a note that was mailed along with the notice to every employer inviting them to call my office. I secured a toll-free number that would be easy to remember and the tax notices went out with the following invitation:

GOT A PROBLEM?
I'M YOUR NEW COMMISSIONER.
I, TOO, HAVE BEEN A TEXAS EMPLOYER
AND I AM HERE TO HELP YOU.
CALL ME AT 1-800-TEC-MARY.

I was looking forward to getting a few calls, untangling some red tape, making people happy, and talking to my fellow business people about my mission to help them be more productive and profitable.

As soon as the notices arrived in mailboxes across the state, the agency switchboard was slammed. In fact, there were so many incoming calls—all for me—that the volume overloaded the agency's telecommunications system. It continued like that for weeks. We kept the toll-free number and used it for years as a way for people to get past the red tape to solve a problem.

My second initiative was greeted quite differently— we took government on a road trip. We created the Texas Business Council, a group made up of representatives from the state's ten largest agencies. Five times a year, several dozen public officials would put on a one-day conference in a different part of the state. Business owners were able to attend and talk to public officials, ask regulatory questions, get face-to-face help with problems, and learn about state resources available to them.

Both the business community and the agencies were enthusiastic, and for the next eight years I spent many days and nights traveling and listening to employers, offering advice and resources, answering questions, and handing out literature. Through the Business Council, which is still operating today, we built trusting relationships between business and government that became collaborations instead of confrontations.

Shortly after Democrat Ann Richards was elected governor, she offered me an even bigger challenge—to fill an empty seat on the Texas Railroad Commission. The state's most powerful, complex, and political regulatory agency, it was an enormous tangle of rules and regulations.

For the next two years, the two other commissioners and I issued rulings affecting $65 billion of the state's economy—principally the energy and transportation industries—in coordination with federal agencies. The workload was staggering and the learning curve steep, but I decided to run for election when my term was up in 1994. A Republican wave swept the country and I was defeated, along with Governor Richards.

I entered public service believing that, like any other

With the late Gov. Ann Richards, as a Texas Railroad commissioner.

enterprise, government's customers have a right to good service and that its shareholders—taxpayers—have a right to efficient and professional management. To accomplish those goals, government needs to work well with the private sector.

Government needs the private sector to achieve its goals, but collaborations between them are often problematic.

My ten years in government taught me that collaborations between these profoundly different cultures, with missions that seem in opposition to each other, are too often problematic and occasionally the cause of serious disruptions of essential services. Whether it's the Internet or the interstate, there's hardly a public entity that hasn't experienced a crisis because of a miscommunication or misunderstanding.

Within weeks of leaving the Railroad Commission, I launched a consulting practice with a single employee—a trusted executive assistant who left with me. I hung out a sign and mailed a letter to government contractors saying, in effect, "Having problems with government? Call me… I can help!"

Within the first few weeks, Northrop Grumman and AT&T became my first clients and have remained with me ever since. Along the way I recruited a team of consultants, all former public service executives, including former executives of the largest state agencies as well as those from cities, counties, and universities.

Instead of selling business to government, our mission has been to help some of the world's largest contractors invent profitable, efficient solutions for government. In some cases that's led to vendors finding solutions or cost savings where it was assumed none were possible. The best measure of our success since 1995 is that this solutions-driven approach is becoming the new best practice in government procurement.

Not since the Technological Revolution[1] has entrepreneurial energy played such a big role in reshaping the business of government. State and federal agencies—from state motor vehicle departments to the Social Security Administration—are no longer just buying software packages for their web portals. Virtually every jurisdiction is working with vendors to invent specific solutions. Yet we've only just begun. Innovation in government is a work in progress, which means there is plenty of room for businesses with good ideas and effective execution.

My ten years of public service in an executive role in one of the largest and fastest growing states in the country—under two Democratic governors and one Republican—allowed me to observe and become an expert in understanding how all levels of government actually operate, under shifting political conditions. As an entrepreneur, I never stopped looking at every government challenge as an opportunity to make institutions more efficient and responsive.

At Strategic Partnerships, Inc. (SPI), we help companies identify public needs they can efficiently and profitably fulfill and show them how to become government's problem solvers and trusted partners. In the process, we're also helping government executives make the most of their relationships with vendors. We are often, in effect, cultural translators.

When the economy began to fall apart in 2007 and 2008, I knew from my experience in government that public officials at all levels would quickly exhaust the easy fixes for yawning

---

1 Also known as the Second Industrial Revolution, roughly from the end of the Civil War until the start of World War I.

budget gaps and be left with options for which there would be no political support—raising taxes and floating more debt. Without massive federal assistance, the only route left would be to turn to the private sector to privatize, outsource, and/or form public-private partnerships.

This is a trend that has been developing for some time, but the Great Recession has accelerated interest and activity. It seemed the perfect time to put what I've learned into book form. A "how to sell to government" approach would have been easy but, having lived in both worlds, I wanted to speak to both sides. If nothing else, I felt I could help business executives and public officials understand each other better and find common ground. I wanted to help make collaborations more successful because I believe public-private partnerships will be critical to our continued economic prosperity as a nation.

The book you hold in your hands is the compilation of what I learned about working with public officials and large government contracting firms, creating successful public-private partnerships, and developing winning business strategies that resonate with diverse stakeholders.

Collaboration Nation aspires to play a role in the debate about how our public institutions can best weather the current financial storm and how we can best reform the business of government for the long haul.

Mary Scott Nabers
Austin, Texas 2012

Collaboration
NATION

HOW PUBLIC-PRIVATE VENTURES
ARE REVOLUTIONIZING THE
BUSINESS OF GOVERNMENT

PART ONE

Bridge Building

1 A Generational Shift

The economic downturn of the past few years is reshaping America's businesses and is also changing forever the way government operates. At every jurisdictional level, public agencies are starving for the funding and resources required to deliver essential services. Hardly a day goes by that a government entity somewhere isn't proposing privatizing some public obligation.

In early 2012, the city of Philadelphia was exploring selling its municipally owned gas utility, the largest in the nation; North Carolina was looking for a private partner to take over the state's three public aquariums and a zoo; and Sacramento, California, officials were planning to lease the city's parking facilities to a private operator to raise money for a new sports and event complex.

Public officials who have run out of other options are increasingly reaching out to private sector partners for capital, expertise, and professional services.

That the federal government has been spending more

than it collects each year is well known, and the fact that Social Security and Medicare are crises in waiting has been a central issue in the national debate for decades. Less apparent until the Great Recession was the scope of financial problems at the state and local levels.

The states alone are estimated to be short $3 trillion in what is needed just to pay future benefits to retired public employees. Local governmental entities have the same problem. Cities throughout America are struggling to find ways to avoid being pushed into bankruptcy.

Critical infrastructure maintenance and upgrades to essential public facilities will cost trillions more. Health care reform, population growth, and education funding will exacerbate the problem. It is a discomfiting picture with no easy solutions. Kicking the can down the road is no longer an option.

Solving this crisis will require the same sort of imagination and collaboration that helped America win World War II.

This crisis took a generation or so to develop, and solving it may take another. It will require the same sort of imagination and collaboration that helped America win World War II, when we converted our manufacturing might from cars to tanks, from lipstick cases to bullets.

The process has already begun. Over the past several years, innovative public-private collaborations have been springing up across the country, merging the interests and obligations of government with the energy and creativity of private enterprise.

An Outbreak of Collaboration

States have entered into public-private partnerships (called P3s) with companies to operate toll roads, build bridges, repair aging government facilities, and manage technology services. Cities are partnering with firms that construct multigenerational activity centers, health care clinics and public safety facilities.

A number of cities have found private sector partners to manage public transportation systems. Public universities are partnering with developers who build hotels, student housing, and sports facilities and then develop retail nearby to offset some of the costs and provide ongoing revenue streams. Private sector partners are lining up to design, build, and operate sports complexes, convention centers, and municipal water treatment plants.

These types of collaborations range from the mundane to the inventive. For example, Chicago leased its parking meters to a private operating company in exchange for a large upfront payment, effectively moving public employees onto private payrolls.

The Texas Education Agency entered into a high-tech partnership with the *New York Times* to create a web portal—Project Share—that links public school teachers throughout the state. The website allows educators to download teaching materials and to share ideas and tools. In a state that spends more than $20 billion a year on education, Project Share costs Texas less than $4 million a year. Not only does it yield productivity gains, the arrangement makes the *New York Times*, including its archives back to 1852, available to nearly five million children. The *Times*, meanwhile, gets the chance to introduce itself to a new generation of potential subscribers.

The P3 concept is not new. In the UK and Canada, governments have been using P3s regularly since the early

1990s. Use of them in the US has taken longer to catch on because in most jurisdictions enabling legislation must first be written and adopted.

An example of a very successful public-private collaboration was completed in 2001 in Washington, DC. The city got a much-needed new school building—the James F. Oyster Bilingual Elementary School—at no public cost in exchange for giving a developer the right to build an apartment house on adjacent city land that had been fallow for many years.

Experts predict more collaborations like this as elected officials find dormant assets that may have been on the public ledgers for a century or more and could be sold, leased, or leveraged. Think tanks like the Reason Foundation are lobbying state legislatures to conduct comprehensive inventories of all public lands and buildings so they can be actively managed—leased, utilized, or divested and returned to the tax rolls.

Taking Stock of Government

There has never been an urgency, until now, for governments to compile comprehensive asset inventory analyses, but the concept is now considered a best practice. In much the same way that businesses and consumers have been deleveraging and selling off unneeded and passive assets, the federal government has proposed putting on the market the estimated 14,000 buildings it owns. The Congressional Office of Management and Budget estimates selling that much real estate could yield $15 billion over three years. The White House Budget Office has estimated that there are another 55,000 federally owned buildings that are dormant or underutilized that also could be sold.

Critics who contend that government is too large are right when it comes to the management of public properties. Government, at all jurisdictional levels, holds unproductive and moribund assets that could be leased, sold, or better managed. Many of those assets are of interest to private sector firms.

This trend toward public-private collaboration in America is inevitable and expected to accelerate, although public officials are still learning how to work with the available tools and sometimes have to adjust for unexpected outcomes.

Some states that sold or leased their toll roads discovered that as the economy soured, traffic declined and revenues fell short of projections.

A few cities built golf courses and other recreational facilities as quality-of-life attractions and later discovered that membership fees didn't cover operational costs. They ended up leasing or selling the properties to private firms.

The public sector marketplace will experience a growth spurt that could put trillions in public spending in play.

One thing is certain—the historically large public sector marketplace is about to experience a growth spurt that will put trillions of dollars of public spending in play. Getting it right will be a challenge, but the potential for success far outweighs the risk. The American economy and quality-of-life for millions of American citizens hang in the balance.

We've Been Here Before

In many ways, collaborations and partnerships between the public and private sectors being initiated today reflect a return to our roots, completing a full circle. For example, many of the toll roads that cities have recently sold or leased were built by private companies during the Revolutionary War and taken over by government in the last century.

As government increasingly looks to private enterprise to help solve problems and deliver public services, it's worth recalling that the United States was settled and built by entrepreneurs. All of America's struggles since have, in one way or another, centered on the shifting balance between private profit and social obligation.

Government contracting practices have historically ebbed and flowed in response to emergencies like war, economic disaster, or a critical mission such as exploring space. These cycles are said by historians to have begun in Boston in 1700s when private investors built America's first public water systems. In the two-plus centuries since, private companies built our canals, railroads, electric grids, urban transit systems, roadways, and ports.

Outsourcing the Revolutionary War

At the beginning of the Revolutionary War, America's navy consisted of a handful of ships commissioned by the colonies and crewed by volunteers. To bulk up, the Continental Congress issued licenses to entrepreneurs willing to operate armed ships and attack British merchant vessels in exchange for a lion's share of the money and goods they recovered. The fleet of privateers was so successful at intercepting British vessels and capturing their cargoes that historians consider the campaign a deciding factor in the war's outcome and a crucial source of investment capital for the new nation.

Our modern system of super highways began in the 1790s with the privately financed building of the Philadelphia and Lancaster Turnpike, predecessor of today's Pennsylvania Turnpike.

One of the most important public-private collaborations in American history was launched in 1843 when Congress voted to underwrite the $30,000 cost of Samuel Morse's first experimental telegraph line from Baltimore to Washington. The telegraph was as revolutionary in its day as the Internet was 150 years later, and an equally powerful engine of economic growth.

Until the 1930s, city transit systems and electricity grids were operated primarily by private companies.

Until the 1930s, city transit systems and electricity grids were operated primarily by private companies under exclusive government franchises. The Great Depression drove many of these privately-owned, essential public service companies into bankruptcy and they were taken over by government agencies

At the same time, President Franklin Roosevelt's New Deal programs created thousands of jobs with mega-projects like the Tennessee Valley Authority and the National Electrical Grid, considered one of the most successful public-private partnerships in US History.

How World War II Changed the Equation

World War II sealed government's role as lead provider of public services, a role that manifested itself in every corner of the country beginning in the 1950s with the buildout of the toll-free interstate highway system. Postwar government at every level expanded in size, influence, and control. The next inflection point in the cycle came in the 1980s when, during another financial crisis, President Ronald Reagan declared, "Government is not the solution to our problems; government is the problem."

Reagan's remark was controversial and confrontational, portraying government as the enemy of prosperity, creating a political climate that was anything but collaborative. While it's true that government and business operate in different worlds, it is counterproductive to think of them as combatants.

Since the 1980s, which saw high-level scandals in contracting at the Defense Department, the debate about what functions government should and shouldn't be involved in has expanded. That debate has accelerated in the past decade as the national debt surged and the Great Recession deflated the economy.

New configurations for government contracting began to appear in the early 1990s. Congress enacted the Intermodal Surface Transportation Efficiency Act (ISTEA), providing a way to combine federal, state, local, private, and toll funding into public-private partnerships formed to improve and expand highway infrastructure. Meanwhile, contracting and ethics rules that had long prohibited architects from providing construction services were relaxed. That cleared the way for more "design-build" projects, where a general contractor is selected to oversee all subcontractors for the design and construction of a facility.

New York Buys a Bridge

Budget crunches and a weak public finance market have been catalysts for innovation, and today all sorts of creative collaborations are changing the way government provides services. For the first time in more than a century, a major highway link in New York City—the Goethals Bridge between Staten Island and New Jersey—is on track to be financed, built, and maintained by a private company. The project is expected to be privately financed, with investors to be repaid in installments over thirty years. The last time a major New York infrastructure project was funded this way was the Brooklyn Bridge, completed in 1883.

By some estimates, New York State will need $250 billion in infrastructure upgrades in the next decade.

"We are buying a bridge… and getting a guaranteed warranty on it," a Port Authority spokesman explained. By some estimates, New York State will need some $250 billion in infrastructure upgrades over the next decade or so. If the Goethals project is a success, many other projects are expected to be similarly structured.

The Port Authority, a bistate agency, needed no new laws to allow it to structure the Goethals contract as a partnership. The legal authority to enter into such partnerships varies from state to state. Some already have laws on the books and others are in the process of enacting enabling legislation.

In New Jersey, the Privatization Task Force was created to develop a long-term approach to shedding some of the

The first step is understanding the very different rules of engagement by which each partner plays.

functions that government can no longer underwrite. Illinois has outsourced management of its state lottery system. West Virginia privatized its nearly bankrupt workers' compensation system. Arizona and Florida, among others, have established councils on efficient government that identify, implement, and/or manage public-private partnerships and the privatization of government activities.

Texas hopes to consolidate all state offices currently scattered around the capital city of Austin into a single downtown campus that would be developed, constructed, and maintained by a private entity. The initial plan calls for land to be set aside for commercial office and retail space that will generate revenue to help offset the state's multidecade lease payments.

There is no doubt that the marriage of public interest and private profit is more than a good idea. It is the future. Those who cite past failures and cost overruns to argue against the merits of this trend are correct that, 235 years after the Declaration of Independence, the business of government is still a work in progress. We continue to strive for that more perfect union, with results that are sometimes uneven.

"Projects or initiatives that underperform or fail to meet expectations should be considered in context," says Jim Ray, a transportation consultant who served in the Office of Management and Budget under President George W. Bush. "We wouldn't do design-build projects today the way we did twenty-five years ago. We've learned how to perform better."

To perform better, business executives and public

officials must learn to work together better. Having lived in both worlds, I know how hard it is to bridge the culture gap between them. The first step is understanding the rules of engagement.

The content, the lessons learned, and the advice provided in the following pages are the sum total of thousands of hours spent working with both public and private sector executives. Whether you are one or the other, a policymaker, or an interested citizen, chances are you'll be surprised by what you learn here and, hopefully, understand how we can collaborate our way back to prosperity.

2 Rethinking The Process

The business of government is undergoing a rapid transformation and will never be the same as it was before the Great Recession. Government can no longer afford to operate the way it has for the past three-quarters of a century.

How well we perform as a nation in the next decade or so will depend on how well business and government collaborate on the inevitable transfer of an estimated $3-$6 trillion in government operations to private and semiprivate entities. The challenge will be to find creative, efficient, and profitable ways to continue providing services.

Politics is the fulcrum for this balancing act, requiring both the public and private sectors to work together to win the trust and support of citizen-customers. It will be a challenging task, especially when taxpayers discover there are no cheap or easy answers. Politicians must be willing to take on risk, champion unproven initiatives, challenge government workers, reach out to contractors, acknowledge taxpayers, and communicate clearly and convincingly through the media to the public at large.

The corporate community must be willing to invest capital, time, and resources to ensure successful collaborations with government. Public-private partnerships are the country's best option for maintaining our economic stability and our global status.

Government no longer has the luxury of providing valuable services at or below cost, and the adjustments that have to be made are already causing discomfort. Examples include the rise in highway tolls in Indiana and parking fees in Chicago following privatization. Public protests and fierce debate have been fanned by a patriotic response to the idiosyncrasies of modern finance. In exchange for an up-front payment of $3.8 billion, the Indiana Toll Road was leased for a term of seventy-five years to an investment group controlled by entities in Australia and Spain.

The transaction was either "the best deal since Manhattan was sold for beads," as Indiana Governor Mitch Daniels declared, or a short-sighted "outsourcing [of] political will," in the words of Oregon Congressman Peter DeFazio, a senior member of the House Transportation and Infrastructure Committee.

However you view such arrangements, they are manifestations of the dire straits in which government executives, especially at the state and local levels, find themselves. It's only going to worsen in the next couple of years as cuts on the federal level filter down.

Public institutions lack the options afforded business, to shed or shutter unsustainable operations, liquidate lines of business, restructure, or recapitalize. The government toolkit contains a set of far more complex options including privatization, outsourcing, shared and managed services, public-private partnerships, and agency consolidations.

Rethinking Reactive Thinking

This is a new world for public officials and for many of the contractors who sell to and work with them. It requires a new way of thinking about how government delivers services. The traditional model has long been the reactive approach—a government agency publishes a Request for Offers (RFO), Request For Information (RFI), or Request For Proposal (RFP) and companies submit formal responses and pricing based on strict specifications.

If procurement officials are more concerned about process than result, vendors focus on process, often at the expense of result.

The reactive approach assumes that a government entity knows exactly what it needs and how it should be delivered; that potential bidders will step forward with what is required; and that they will deliver on time and on budget. The biggest problem with this process is that once a formal call for bids has been published, the law typically prohibits communications between potential bidders and the prospective government customer. There is no opportunity to discuss options, explore alternatives, or investigate funding and pricing options.

If the purchase is as prosaic as 10,000 tons of road salt, the traditional model tends to work well—the low bid is probably going to win and the prospects of success are high. But when it comes to major projects—technology purchases, data management systems, infrastructure repairs, upgrading communications networks—the reactive approach, defined by exacting procedures that discourage collaboration or alternative options, are usually adversarial and inefficient. There is no mechanism that allows for innovation and problem solving.

When procurement officials are more concerned about process than results, vendors have no choice but to focus on the process, often at the expense of result.

The High Cost of Process

It is too easy under the reactive approach to win the battle while losing the war. One of the more recent examples of a failed traditional procurement occurred in Texas, where the state requested bids to consolidate the data centers of twenty-eight agencies. IBM was the successful bidder, projecting a cost savings to the state of about $750 million.

The procurement was doomed for many reasons, not least of which was the almost complete lack of communication between the parties during the process, leaving each to make their own assumptions. The process provided no way for technology vendors to submit alternative methods of delivering the services. The state's procurement document required vendors to bid to exact specifications and service levels.

The consolidation effort ran into problems early. IBM later reported that some of the agencies "failed to cooperate" because "ceding control of their individual environments in favor of a centralized, common system was dangerous and unrealistic."

For its part, the state would later cite IBM for what it claimed were "chronic failures." In August 2010, the state's technology agency announced it was looking for new contractors to finish the job. IBM may have followed the process, but neither party could call the contract a success.

The case illustrates what happens when government agencies and vendors are restricted by the traditional bidding process from discussing all the options and challenges in a major procurement.

The price of admission is a huge disincentive for firms to compete for government business.

By contrast, the proactive approach, gaining traction on an agency-by-agency basis, begins with brainstorming discussions with potential vendors before drafting a Request For Proposal and in some cases running test or pilot programs to get real-time data to analyze. The final bidding process remains competitive, but the goals are better defined so that the government customer and the successful private vendor are more likely to end up with a mutual win.

Another factor driving the proactive approach is that companies want to reduce the staggering costs of preparing bid documents for large government contracts. Preparing a bid gets expensive when the request is for custom solutions that require bidders to develop custom products, test them to make sure they'll work as intended, then design custom support. All of this takes place under onerous bidding terms and conditions.

For major undertakings, vendor companies report the outlay can easily reach $2 million per bid, with no certainty of success. If there are five bidders for a $100 million opportunity, that's $10 million spent by private firms before the contract's even been awarded, $8 million of which produces no business for the also-rans. The price of admission

is a huge disincentive for firms to compete for government business.

The emerging proactive model begins with public officials asking about solutions that might be available in the marketplace. Unfortunately, this approach remains the exception because government purchasers are often uncomfortable straying from tradition.

From Best Price to Best Value

Public officials no longer make most procurement decisions based on price alone. Best value is the new standard. Getting there, however, can sometimes be a challenge. Vendors often complain that agency officials write RFPs that describe a Maserati with a budget that covers the price of a Hyundai. Companies that bid on such contracts may be inclined to ignore the risks just to capture, or "buy," the business, and the outcome usually suffers.

It's not uncommon in situations like this for companies to discover after the fact that they lack the resources to deliver even the minimum. They go into the bidding process thinking they'll find a way to squeeze out a profit once they get the contract. That can work in the private sector where process is less important than profit, but public sector contracts are usually specific and ironclad. Deviation from an original agreement with a public entity is often greeted with dismay, distrust, and disputes—all in full public view.

Experienced contractors who want to reduce risk and increase the chance of success do their homework before submitting any bid document. They approach each opportunity with care and deliberation.

A veteran government sales representative for a Fortune 100 vendor put it this way:

We try to position ourselves not as the low-cost provider but the best-value, sustainable provider. If we feel we thoroughly understand what's wanted and are comfortable about the process that will be used to evaluate our performance, we're more likely to participate. But if it's a case where the public entity put together an RFP in a vacuum without an identifiable path to success, we'll almost always choose to ignore it rather than invest the time and resources required to put together a bid.

When the private sector is discouraged from innovating solutions for public customers, we all lose.

The next step in the evolution of public-private ventures is for government officials to do more to involve potential private sector partners in the planning process before bids are solicited. More collaboration between public and private executives will inevitably result in better outcomes.

3 Turning Customers Into Partners

O utsourcing became widespread in the commercial sector in the 1990s, but many government officials held back, wary of surrendering even limited control of public services to private firms. In a perfect world, there is an argument to be made that career civil servants, who understand the mechanics of government and are directly responsible to their constituencies, are best qualified to deliver results. In the real and imperfect world, government execs know that outsourcing, privatization, and public-private partnerships often offer the best, most efficient, and in some cases inevitable solutions.

There have been some demonstrable successes that give public leaders confidence in public-private partnerships. In the years since 1996, when Kansas privatized its child welfare system, the number of children in foster care has been halved, the number of adoptions has doubled, and a federal study gave the state an above-average score among thirty-two states for protecting children and preserving families.

The evidence of success in public-private ventures is often the absence of controversy and media attention.

Massachusetts passed a law to allow private agents such as the Automobile Association of America (AAA) to provide vehicle registration and related services that had only been available through public motor vehicle agency offices. In 2010, in spite of a million new registrations and 2.5 million renewals, Massachusetts officials reported they were able to close eight satellite offices.

The evidence of success in public-private ventures is often the absence of controversy and media attention. Good news doesn't sell as well as bad news so successful public-private collaborative efforts rarely get media attention. Failure, however, tends to grab headlines, so public officials are understandably cautious.

One well-publicized misfire was the outsourcing by the IRS of about $1 billion in collections from individual taxpayers who owed the government less than $25,000. Government downsizings had shrunk IRS staff so much that the agency did not have the resources to handle the labor-intensive collecting in-house. Congress approved outsourcing the task and contractors competing for the work were to be paid through fees of up to 25 percent of revenue collected. It seemed like a wise, pragmatic, entrepreneurial solution.

However, at the end of the second year, the IRS reported program costs exceeded the $49 million collected. In the ensuing debate over what went wrong, Democratic Senator Byron Dorgan called the program "the hood ornament for incompetence." A leading House Republican, Representative

Jim Ramstad, countered that stopping the program before it had a chance to evolve meant none of the delinquent $1 billion would ever be recovered.

The collections experiment at the IRS was tiny compared to the overall operations of the agency, but this highly visible embarrassment reverberated in one way or another in every statehouse, courthouse, and city hall. Public-sector executives are generally conscientious professionals and contentious public debate over unsuccessful initiatives has a chilling effect on their willingness to try new things.

Understanding Public Officials

To understand the culture of government marketplaces, vendors must be able to relate to the people who live and work there. For example, the tactics that get a sales rep a meeting with a potential commercial sector customer are almost always inappropriate or ineffective in the public sector. Securing meetings with executives at the senior level of government is difficult.

Many company executives believe that hiring a lobbyist is the best approach to getting government contracts. Lobbyists have their place in relationships between business and government, but executives in every government jurisdiction resent lobbyists who use heavy-handed measures such as contacting elected officials to secure meetings. Meetings are best arranged by individuals who have strong relationships with executive staff. Those who have served in government know the backlash that often results when lobbyists are involved.

Lobbyists are hired to influence legislation, not procurement. Their networks consist of elected officials, legislative staffs, and experts in policy and budget. They rarely

Lobbyists may be persuasive communicators, but few understand the rules and mechanics of procurement.

meet with agency executives, program directors, IT managers, and other stakeholders who make procurement recommendations. Few lobbyists have sales or marketing training. They may be persuasive communicators, but few understand the rules and mechanics of procurement, which are outlined in detail in Part Two of this book.

A competent lobbying firm can usually secure a meeting with a government executive but nothing annoys professional civil servants more than having them do so through an elected official. Confident government executives may push back but most will simply agree to a vendor meeting and then resent for a long time feeling manipulated. The results of this approach are predictably dismal.

Tighter ethics rules have further diminished the effectiveness of involving elected officials in this process. As transparency in government has increased, elected officials have become increasingly wary of meddling in any procurement issue for fear of inadvertently crossing a legal boundary, or exposing themselves to political problems.

Public officials also respond poorly to tactics such as consultative selling: "Tell me what your problems are and what keeps you up at night." Public officials lack the time and the desire to educate company reps. They want to hear about solutions, innovations, and options that might address some of their immediate problems and they expect vendors to understand their issues and challenges.

Public executives want vendors to treat them as partners

and equals. They resent anyone who acts like a know-it-all, name-drops, or expresses regional, cultural, or political prejudices. Agency heads who hold the purse strings are seasoned professionals with a constituency they care about and strive to serve as effectively as possible.

Procurement officials may not be innovators, entrepreneurs, or captains of industry, but they are CEOs, COOs, and CFOs. They don't get big bonuses at the end of the year, but they run some of the biggest investment houses, engineering firms, health care complexes, and educational institutions in the world. They want their suppliers to treat them as valued, long-term clients and professionals.

The Public-Private Culture Divide

Entrepreneurs and companies new to the process of competing for government business hold many other misconceptions about the public sector. Just as it is difficult to understand European culture if one has never traveled outside the United States, it is hard to understand the government marketplace if one has no experience in it.

It is this cultural divide that creates much of the stress and apprehension about partnering between the two sectors. Successful collaboration requires commitment from both parties along with patience, good communications, transparency, respect, and knowledge sharing.

Some of the principal challenges in government procurement include:

- Capturing government contracts involves selling into a political environment—politics must be taken into account.
- Information gathering is critical and the sales team with the most information usually wins.

- Public sector procurement is highly structured.
- Sales cycles are longer but contracts are written for numerous years.
- There are many stakeholders involved in decision-making and each stakeholder is important.
- Contract negotiating takes place within rigid guidelines.
- Public officials are risk-averse decision makers who look for experience, references, credibility, and solutions that appear safe.
- Communication between buyers and sellers is often inadequate.

Understanding public-sector culture starts with gathering information: historical knowledge about the governmental entity, awareness of the politics surrounding a contracting opportunity, and a basic understanding of specific budget issues.

Most private sector firms fear the politics of selling to government, but politics is as unavoidable a factor as price. Final contracting decisions are rarely driven directly by politics, but going into the process without understanding alliances, interest groups, and even power struggles can be frustrating at best. For that reason alone, it is important to study the political landscape before trying to enter it.

A Multitude of Stakeholders

One of the biggest differences between commercial and government business is the number and diversity of stakeholders who can be involved in purchasing decisions. Building a school may involve a great deal of public debate by parents and taxpayers who can influence outcomes. Outsourcing a city's parking meters often requires a strong public relations effort to explain changes in parking rules and fees necessary to make the procurement profitable.

Sales cycles take longer in public sector marketplaces but contracts are written for numerous years.

The vendors that government executives like to deal with are those who identify all the stakeholders and are prepared to build the consensus necessary for success. That includes considering competitors, teaming partners, budget, history of the initiative, and the level of public interest. Nine times out of ten, the team with the most information about a project wins the contract.

Public sector procurement is highly structured. Even in P3 engagements, contracting issues are rigid. Robust record keeping and reporting and adherence to rules are often the prime factors by which a procurement will be judged. Contractors should respect the process even though it may seem inefficient at times, but also be confident enough to ask the right questions in a way that is professional and on point.

Everyone in a leadership role in government service is overworked these days. Most will tell you that they have little patience for vendor reps who do things like take up their time asking for information they could have downloaded from a website or looked up in the official records.

Long Sales Cycles and Long Tails

Sales cycles take longer in public sector marketplaces but are balanced by the fact that contracts are written for numerous years and contractors who provide quality services and/or products are usually difficult to unseat. Government partners are loyal to contractors who perform well. They tend to resist change and that tendency often results in numerous contract extensions. Government contracts can have very long tails.

Finally, terms and conditions in good contracts are quite different from those found in commercial contracts. Some standard contract language will trigger alarm bells when reviewed by corporate risk managers, and many a contract has run aground because of a liquidated damages clause. Negotiating the details can be exasperating because public sector attorneys often have little authority to negotiate aggressively.

Cooperative Purchasing Programs

Many governmental organizations have found alternative procurement methods that are quicker, more efficient, and less cumbersome. The most popular and least controversial are cooperative purchasing programs. Firms that participate in these programs can avoid a long and costly procurement process.

For example, an association, state, or federal government sponsors the cooperative program, which evaluates products, services, and pricing for its member agencies. Companies are vetted and then are allowed to sell products and services directly to co-op members without having to go through a competitive procurement process.

A county purchasing agent in need of mobile phones, for instance, can find offerings from approved telecom suppliers and in many cases can negotiate directly for custom features. Purchases can be made quickly and efficiently since discounted pricing has already been negotiated.

Another less common alternative purchasing option is called a shared contract. Public officials are allowed to buy products or services off a contract that another governmental entity has agreed to share. A shared contract can be used by multiple governmental entities. Usually it is up to a contractor to explain to the buyer that a shared contract exists and offer it as an option.

Numerous states have cooperative programs for IT purchases. State agencies are usually required to purchase technology through that program or justify an exemption that would trump the fact that the state's CIO has personally overseen the process of vetting IT services, products, and pricing.

Outsourcing, privatizing, and partnerships will generate thousands of new jobs in the private sector.

Federal schedules are accepted in most states, allowing public buyers to make purchases based on federal terms.

P3s and The Law

Finally, information gathering should include state statutes governing public-private partnerships and any background data related to similar engagements.

For major capital projects like the $1 billion replacement for the Goethals Bridge between Staten Island and New Jersey, the future clearly belongs to public-private partnerships—P3s. Fortunately, there is a world of experience to draw on when government considers a P3 method of procurement. Australia, Canada, and the UK, among many other nations, have been using the P3 engagement structure for decades.

In the US, P3s are relatively new but the trend is well established. Many states have statutes that allow and encourage P3s, and many are in the process of writing enabling legislation. Each state's approach may differ slightly and the details may be minor but are essential to know and understand.

Toward a Virtuous Circle

Growth in the public sector marketplace will continue to accelerate in the near future. Companies of all sizes are eligible to participate and prime contractors aggressively seek well-positioned and capable subcontractors to be a part of the overall team.

Outsourcing, privatizing, partnerships, and large government contracts will generate thousands of new jobs in the private sector. Jobs will move from public to private payrolls as public entities outsource more service delivery.

The best outcome would be a virtuous circle: government becomes more innovative and efficient and delivers better public services; a fresh source of capital flows into P3 initiatives, stimulating economic vigor and hiring; and the resulting increased tax revenues will underwrite the cost of reinventing government for the benefit of all citizens and taxpayers.

PART TWO

Collaborating

4 ★ P3s: Wave of the Present

A silver lining of the Great Recession is that government officials have had to become more discerning about which services can or should only be delivered by a public agency and which services and infrastructure might be more efficiently financed, delivered, and maintained in one form or another by the private sector. One of the painful lessons of the economic crisis is that projects that sound good in principle during flush economic times can quickly turn into financial catastrophes when tax or use revenues fail to meet projections.

One of the more notable cases is the 2004 Harrisburg, Pennsylvania, waste-recovery project that in 2011 precipitated the city ending up in state receivership. The agency responsible for operating the state capital's incinerator gave a contract to a vendor in 2004 to substantially upgrade the plant, where solid waste was burned for energy. The vendor had done smaller projects before, but nothing the size of the Harrisburg procurement. The winning bid was 30 percent below the next lowest entry.

The litany of things that went wrong covers numerous institutions and stakeholders but basically the vendor couldn't complete the job for the price quoted. Cost overruns, coupled with overoptimistic revenue projections, unwise financing, and an economic tsunami, converged to trigger a financial crisis that left the city unable to pay its bills.

Harrisburg has had plenty of company in struggling with its debt. Between 2005 and 2010, state and local governments increased their outstanding debt obligations by about a third, just as the fading economy was taking its bite out of tax revenue. That's how we ended up with an estimated $3 trillion shortfall in state and local budgets nationwide. We've been here before, but this time—with the federal government unable to step in—we have no choice but to reinvent how the people's business gets done.

From Contractor to Collaborator

Previously, a state, city, or county planning to build a new stretch of highway or a school often chose to finance it through municipal bonds or other public finance vehicles and then controlled the project by acting, in effect, as general contractor. The downside of this traditional model— government as the general contractor—becomes apparent when there are problems with the design or build aspects, as happened in Harrisburg. When a public entity is the general contractor, there is no shared risk—government is ultimately responsible.

Increasingly, public officials are choosing instead to enter into what is known as a design-build procurement. A quasi-public-private partnership is launched and the partners work shoulder to shoulder, but the public entity is not the general contractor. Most of that risk is shifted to the private sector partner, allowing government employees to focus on oversight while continuing to deliver on core obligations.

When a public entity is the general contractor, there is no shared risk—government is ultimately responsible.

The third option is rapidly redefining the role of government—true public-private partnerships, or P3s. P3s have been used in other parts of the world for many years, but are just beginning to become the new standard in the US.

In a P3, the private sector partner invests equity and shoulders the financial risk. The public entity guarantees the private partner a revenue stream. Or the agreement may call for an operation-driven payout of some type over a period of many years, typically two or more decades. P3s have been used to build toll roads, airports, and other infrastructure projects that are financed by private capital and repaid from operating revenue. Now, P3s are being used for all types of government initiatives.

P3s are gaining a wide following because the public finance markets have been weak, tax revenues are recovering slowly in most places, governments have downsized and don't have the staffs they once did, and there is strong political resistance to the risks associated with adding costly projects and obligations to overburdened public balance sheets.

Before the economic crisis, the question was, "*How* would you like to procure your new facility?" Today, increasingly, the question is, "*Would* you like to build this new facility by engaging in a public-private partnership or would you prefer to have no facility at all?"

No system is perfect, but P3s are catching on for a common-sense reason: both parties have a stake in the outcome. The private sector is attracted to P3s because the predictability of government revenue holds down borrowing costs. Also, partnerships often contain incentives that reward efficient management and give vendors more control over a project's profitability.

The private sector is attracted to P3s because the inherent stability of government revenue holds down borrowing costs.

Government officials like them because in most instances cost overruns come out of the private partner's pocket, not government's. Done well, a P3 is more economical for government than doing it the old-fashioned way.

A P3 engagement allows public officials to move forward with infrastructure, construction, and other urgent projects that might otherwise have to be delayed until tax revenues rise or the public finance market becomes more accessible. Financial partners with a stake in the long-term outcome will pay close attention to detail, costs, timelines, and expectations. The investment community will provide a level of due diligence—to protect investors—that government rarely can, and capital will flow to those vendors who are the most experienced and credible.

A Look Inside the Hive

Private sector misconception about how government works is a big issue, and it cuts both ways. Public officials sometimes forget that private sector firms have an obligation to earn a competitive return for their investors. As customers, public procurement executives are shielded from the frustration that vendor reps often experience when they come up against a system that seems inefficient and inflexible. Good sales reps get pressure from their own stakeholders, who are accustomed to shorter sales cycles, sales quotas, and quarterly results.

Private sector misconception about how government works is a big issue, and it cuts both ways.

To address this issue, private sector firms should invest time and resources in helping their sales teams and corporate executives understand the world of government. It's the same as training people when entering a new international market—first you become familiar with local culture and customs.

All government agencies are not created equal. Each has its unique cultural differences and even agencies in the same field, such as state departments of transportation, will have cultures and procedures that vary from state to state. With trillions of public dollars on the line in the next few years, it is perplexing how many bidders and vendors fail to do their homework before trying to win government business.

Meet the Stakeholders

Stakeholders in government procurement include elected officials, executive staff, program directors, procurement officers, CFOs, attorneys, and policy analysts. Since many of them will play a role in influencing purchasing and/or contracting decisions, it's important to understand what motivates, excites, worries, and calms them.

The approach to government markets is the same as any foreign market—find a partner who has lived there, speaks the language, knows the culture, and is seen as a member of the community.

Most public officials and stakeholders have had public sector training with well-defined career requirements and are accustomed to close public scrutiny. They operate in a rigid, rules-driven environment and are sensitive to peer influence. In their world, there are no profit margins, quarterly sales quotas, or stock prices. They have been taught to avoid risk and are rewarded and promoted on the basis of seniority, attention to detail, and how well they follow the rules.

What government stakeholders care about most:

- Selecting a "safe" contracting partner;
- Getting the best price/value for taxpayers;
- Never being involved with a failed project;
- Staying out of the press; and
- Having solid justifications for final decisions.

Building trusting relationships with public officials is often difficult. Just getting a meeting can be a challenge. For unknown vendor reps, it may be impossible. There are no easy solutions and no magic bullets, and the practice of hiring lobbyists to assist with contracting efforts is becoming passé.

If the goal is to win a business development meeting with a public official, your best route is usually going to be a procurement consultant who has been a public official in a previous career, has established relationships and credibility, is fluent in the lingo, and is already conversant with the issues your potential customer faces. It's the same approach as when entering a foreign market—you find a partner who has lived there, speaks the language, knows the history and culture, and will be perceived as a member of the community.

5 Transparency and the Trust Dividend

M any practices and assumptions common in business-to-business deals translate poorly when the customer is a public entity. The single most important difference is transparency. Barring a lawsuit, regulatory action, or a required disclosure by a public company, failures within commercial transactions are usually private matters known only to officers and executives. The public rarely hears about contract disputes, cost overruns, management disagreements, losses, and/or unmet expectations.

The opposite is true when it comes to government contracting. Transparency is a way of life for public officials. Every step of a procurement process is meticulously documented and paperwork related to government contracts is available to taxpayers, competitors, and the media. A major contracting failure may land on the front page of the newspaper. Unmet expectations can become a legislative issue.

The second most important difference in contracting

with government is the definition of success and failure. On its most basic level, a commercial transaction is a success when the seller makes an honest profit and the buyer is satisfied. For a government contract to be considered a success, the vendor is expected to finish on time, meet expectations, stay within budget, avoid controversy, and make a profit.

The highest value among public executives in their interactions with vendors is trust, which they bestow with great care.

Failure in a business-to-government transaction can take many forms and the cost of failure to government officials is often steep—budget reductions, loss of oversight responsibilities, and even career setbacks. That's why the highest value among public executives in their interactions with vendors is trust, which they bestow with great care.

The high price of failure along with the risk-averse nature of government decision makers means a contractor's most important skill is knowing how to build trusting relationships. When I was on the government side, I learned how high a premium public execs put on having partners who understand them as people and the unique issues facing their institutions.

In my private sector experiences, I have felt the frustration a contractor feels when confronted with the limitations and the bureaucracy of government. I also identify with the sense of higher purpose and aversion to risk taking that make public officials demanding customers.

Procurement executives tend to be wary in their

communications with potential bidders and with contractors. Their greatest fear is that they will unintentionally share privileged information, do or say anything that could be regarded as an ethics violation, or be perceived as giving one company an unfair advantage over competitors. Most conscientious public officials will err on the side of caution even though that often makes it harder for vendors to get the information they need to prepare good proposals.

Slow and Steady versus Fast and Ready

This hypercaution can verge on paranoia, and sometimes that's exactly what it is. More commonly it's driven by other, unseen forces that are outside the control of the purchasing executive. Being a public procurement official is about as difficult today as it ever has been. With budget constraints likely to be a factor for years to come, there is little relief in sight. For public-private collaborations to be successful, public officials need private sector partners who are forgiving of the system's shortcomings and willing to go the extra mile.

"Being a contracting officer may be the most thankless job in government," says attorney James P. Gallatin, a government contracts expert and the editor of the *Global Regulatory Enforcement Law Blog*.

Gallatin says that after a decade during which the total value of federal contracts more than doubled, "the acquisition workforce has generally remained constant." He explained:

> There is an ever-increasing workload; responsibility for billions of dollars in purchases from sophisticated and highly aggressive commercial vendors across a staggering variety of industries; compensation is far below private sector peers; constant scrutiny

by their agency personnel is common; auditors and Inspectors General use hindsight to judge success; regular second-guessing or simple overruling by senior management is rampant; and there is continual mocking by congressional representatives and senators. Private industry has no choice but to do a better job on its end of supporting contracting officers in creating reasonable, defensible contracts.

> *"Private industry has no choice but to do a better job on its end of supporting contracting officers."*

Private sector partners should know that the pace of government will appear glacial compared to an entrepreneurial culture where communication is instant and decisions can be made quickly with little or no transparency. Companies are managed by fiscal quarters, while government is managed by a fiscal year or in some cases multiple years—and every public transaction is open to outside scrutiny by anyone.

Public execs are traditionalists. Their horizons are distant. Government decision makers are uncomfortable with the urgency and flexibility required to run a successful for-profit firm. People in government are rarely fired for being slow to act. The danger for them lies in acting too quickly or failing to think through every conceivable detail of a situation.

Entrepreneurs will talk about solving problems "by the end of today," while public workers will say, "Let's talk about this again next week."

From Tradition to Innovation

A number of more innovative procurement processes are being tried today, but change has been slow. For example, some officials are experimenting with virtual vendor conferences, which are completely transparent to all participants and often attract interest from more distant contractors. In Part Five of this book, you will find more detailed examples of the sorts of innovations that are taking place in a number of states as well as suggestions about how to get the most out of every vendor conference.

One of the most interesting and encouraging new trends includes unsolicited proposals. In many jurisdictions, legislators have enacted laws that require public executives to review and evaluate all unsolicited proposals. This is a huge departure from what has been the norm. Most such statutes prescribe a timeline for proposal analysis as well as a competitive process if the proposal is deemed viable.

Traditionally, public officials have been discouraged from actively courting the private sector for ideas, but that appears to be changing as well.

When making presentations to, and working with, public officials, there are four basic rules, which are described in more detail in Part Three but can be summarized as follows:

- **Keep it short:** Strictly heed the time allotted for any meeting. Never go over whatever time was given without permission. Present your solution and allow time for questions.
- **Get to the point quickly**: Speak to outcomes, cost estimates, timelines, and examples of how the solution you are offering has worked elsewhere.
- **Keep it simple**: Avoid Power Point slides if

possible. If not, keep them to a handful at most, and don't delve into the details unless asked.

- **Follow through**: At the conclusion, if there is interest, ask about next steps and make sure you know how to follow up after the meeting.

A Case Study in Possibilities

During my career in government, I was involved with an interesting and successful state agency procurement aimed at upgrading and streamlining some document-handling procedures. The budget for the project was $60 million, making it a highly visible procurement. The agency was anxious to get it right and ensure the intended benefits. Having been an entrepreneur, I knew the best solution would come from outside the agency from the private sector.

As an entrepreneur, I know the best solutions tend to come from the private sector.

Before designing a formal solicitation document, I encouraged agency staff to ask a dozen or so potential vendors to suggest a solution and provide cost estimates, timelines, and anticipated outcomes. I knew from my business experience that we were asking a lot of the vendors, and I expected some would walk away rather than commit the resources it would take to comply. However, many were willing to make suggestions and provide options to meet our objectives.

In the end, the process worked well for the agency, resulting in significant cost savings and reduced error rates.

The bid competition was fair because vendors were told to offer whatever type of creative solution they thought would best meet our needs. Since that experience, I've been an advocate for this method of procurement and I've tried hard to encourage government executives to use this model. It seems to me that by explaining goals and outcomes and allowing contractors to decide how they can best achieve the objectives, all parties benefit. It is more costly when government officials force contractors to follow a specific model.

The Trust Dividend

Bad outcomes sow doubt, create skepticism, and engender distrust in public executives. Few career civil servants have experience running a for-profit enterprise. They have no context for dealing with an unsuccessful venture. When a commercial transaction runs into trouble, there is usually some flexibility to make timely course adjustments and accommodations to try to save a profit or a customer. This is not the case in a public procurement where the rules and procedures are meticulously defined and vendors are held to account for all deviations from the terms of a contract.

Private companies seeking their first contracts often do so believing that even if they don't get it just right at first, they can tweak a project to preserve a profit. That's a fundamental mistake. Government projects don't allow for tweaking and public officials don't like to make changes.

Government decision makers will almost always stick with contractors they know and trust rather than take a chance on someone or something new. There is little incentive to take on risk, even if a competing vendor demonstrates another way to do the same job better and/or cheaper.

Competing against an entrenched vendor is often difficult. Unseating an incumbent takes patience, creativity, and relationship building. But the rewards are often multiyear contracts and seamless renewals.

The gulf between public and private sector personalities is beginning to narrow as public-private partnerships become more common. Leaders in both sectors are slowly becoming more knowledgeable about and more forgiving of each other.

At my firm, we hold training courses on a regular basis for public sector decision makers who are interested in understanding private sector vendors better. They come to us because they want to increase competition for their procurements. We show them how to encourage vendor competition, elicit better proposals, encourage innovative solutions, and turn vendors into trusted partners.

On the flip side, we also train vendors who want to be more successful selling to government decision makers. One way we do that is to help companies become more judicious about which contracts to bid on and which entities are good fits for their offerings. It's common in government contracting to win a big job and later pay a high price if the match turns out to have been flawed from the start.

It's common to win a big job and later pay a high price if the match turns out to have been flawed from the start.

PART THREE

Communicating

6 ★ The Lay of the Land

S
uccessful public-private collaborations rarely happen by accident, and the burden of ensuring success falls largely on the shoulders of private sector contractors. In an entrepreneurial system, government is not expected to be the incubator or engine of innovation, but most public officials are eager to hear about solution-centered collaborations, especially with firms that understand and respect the rules of engagement.

The number of stakeholder groups in a public-private venture is exponentially greater than in a commercial transaction, and their interests are often misaligned. The objectives of one group frequently conflict with another. More parties multiplies the risk factors. In doing business with government, those risks are sometimes hard to anticipate and difficult to control.

Furthermore, the outcome of a collaboration may depend on unexpected shifts in the political winds and occasionally on the real thing, as happened after Hurricane

Katrina devastated New Orleans and the Gulf Coast. Some of the contracts that were awarded to provide emergency shelter and other services to survivors were still being debated and litigated years later. However, it is possible to identify many of the risks and to create an atmosphere of trust and mutual respect with public executives so that if an obstacle or problem occurs, resolving it is more likely to be a collaboration instead of a confrontation.

There are some common misconceptions held by companies pursuing public contracts and common mistakes made in preparing proposals and executing contracts. Understanding public officials and learning how to successfully compete in a challenging but potentially rewarding market begins with an understanding of the way governments are structured.

The Civics of Collaboration

Each level of government and each public entity has its own culture. On the federal level, there are common rules that cover all government business, but each agency has its idiosyncrasies. For the purposes of this book, I have focused on state, local, health care, and educational entities where the variations are the greatest and where the opportunities for public-private ventures are growing the fastest:

- State agencies
- Counties
- Cities and municipalities
- Public and charter school districts
- Higher education
- Hospitals and health care complexes

The strategy for developing partnerships is different for each. Different forms of government determine who holds the purse strings and how much of a role is played by politics. For example, government tends to be a more political environment at the county level than at the state, while hospitals and higher education are the least political environments.

Some states have what is known as a cabinet form of government, while others have a strong agency structure. The first step in determining who has budget authority is to find out which form it is and who is the potential partner.

In a cabinet form, the governor appoints every major agency head and those public executives implement and oversee the governor's policies and agenda. In order to work with state agencies operating under this model, business executives need to get buy-in from advisors and policy experts in the governor's office.

In a strong agency form of government, budget authority rests with the person who heads the agency.

On the next four pages are some examples of the forms of government in a selection of jurisdictions, and information about state legislative and budget cycles.

Examples of Forms of Municipal Government

City	Type/Leadership
Los Angeles	City: Governed by mayor and 15-member city council. A mayor-council-commission form of government. Commission members are generally appointed by the mayor and subject to the approval of city council.
San Diego	City: Governed by a mayor and an 8-member city council.
San Jose	City: A council-manager government with a city manager nominated by the mayor and elected by city council.
San Francisco	City and County: Consolidated city-county government. Mayor is also the county executive, and the county board of supervisors acts as the city council. Strong-mayor system.
Fresno	City: Governed by a mayor and a 7-member city council. Fresno is a full-service charter city operating under a strong-mayor system of government.
Jacksonville	City-County: Consolidated government with Duval County. A strong-mayor system with the election of a 19-member city council.
Miami	City: Council-manager system with a mayor-appointed city manager.

Tampa	City: Governed by a mayor and 7-member non-partisan city council. Strong-mayor system.
Chicago	City: Mayor is chief executive, appoints commissioners and other officials who oversee the various departments. City council is the legislative branch, made up of 50 aldermen.
Aurora	City: Mayor-Council
Rockford	City: Mayor-Council
Joliet	City: Council-Manager. City council appoints the manager.
New York	City: Mayor-Council. City council is a unicameral body of 51 members, each elected from a geographic district, normally for four year terms.
Buffalo	City: Mayor-Council
Rochester	City: Mayor-Council
Houston	City: Mayor-Council. All municipal elections in Texas are nonpartisan.
San Antonio	City: Council-Manager The council hires the city manager to handle day to day operations.
Dallas	City: Council-Manager. The council appoints the city manager.

State Governance and Cycles

State	Cabinet Form?	Legislative Cycle	Budget Cycle
Alabama	Yes	Annual	Annual
Alaska	Yes	Annual	Annual
Arizona	Yes	Annual	Annual
Arkansas	Yes	Annual	Annual
California	Yes	Annual	Annual
Colorado	Yes	Annual	Annual
Connecticut	Yes	Annual	Biennial
Delaware	Yes	Annual	Annual
Florida	Yes	Annual	Annual
Georgia	**No**	Annual	Annual
Hawaii	Yes	Annual	Biennial
Idaho	**No**	Annual	Annual
Illinois	Yes	Annual	Annual
Indiana	Yes	Annual	Biennial
Iowa	Yes	Annual	Annual
Kansas	Yes	Annual	Annual
Kentucky	Yes	Annual	Biennial
Louisiana	Yes	Annual	Annual
Maine	Yes	Annual	Biennial
Maryland	Yes	Annual	Annual
Massachusetts	Yes	Annual	Annual
Michigan	Yes	Annual	Annual
Minnesota	Yes	Annual	Biennial

Mississippi	**No**	Annual	Annual
Missouri	Yes	Annual	Annual
Montana	Yes	Biennial	Biennial
Nebraska	Yes	Annual	Biennial
Nevada	**No**	Biennial	Biennial
New Hampshire	**No**	Annual	Biennial
New Jersey	Yes	Annual	Annual
New Mexico	Yes	Annual	Annual
New York	Yes	Annual	Annual
North Carolina	Yes	Annual	Biennial
North Dakota	Yes	Biennial	Biennial
Ohio	Yes	Annual	Biennial
Oklahoma	Yes	Annual	Annual
Oregon	**No**	Annual	Biennial
Pennsylvania	Yes	Annual	Annual
Rhode Island	Yes	Annual	Annual
South Carolina	Yes	Annual	Annual
South Dakota	Yes	Annual	Annual
Tennessee	Yes	Annual	Annual
Texas	**No**	Biennial	Biennial
Utah	Yes	Annual	Annual
Vermont	Yes	Annual	Annual
Virginia	Yes	Annual	Biennial
Washington	Yes	Annual	Biennial
West Virginia	Yes	Annual	Annual
Wisconsin	Yes	Biennial	Biennial
Wyoming	Yes	Annual	Biennial

Why State and Local versus Federal?

The most compelling reason for focusing on state and local jurisdictions is that the budgets are large and, unlike the federal budget, the bulk of the money is spent on current operations and capital outlays. According to the Congressional Office of Management and Budget, only about 10 percent of the current Federal budget of about $3.5 trillion is spent outside of defense (highly specialized), Social Security (direct payments to beneficiaries), interest expense, health care programs (Medicare, Medicaid, etc.), and other safety net programs or entitlements.

Federal expenditures may get the headlines, but it's state and local where the opportunities are greatest for innovation and growth.

By contrast, close to 90 percent of all state and local government general expenditures—about $2.9 trillion in 2010—are categorized by the US Census Bureau as "current operation and capital outlays." A third of that is spent by just four states—California, New York, Texas and Florida.

The federal government's civilian payroll head count is close to 1.5 million, whereas the full-time and equivalent state and local head count is about 16.5 million. Federal expenditures may get the headlines, but it's state and local where the opportunities are greatest for innovation and growth.

Jurisdictions at every level face the most difficult financial crisis since the 1970s, when New York City teetered on the edge of bankruptcy and a headline in the *New York Daily News*—"Ford To New York: Drop Dead"—helped Jimmy Carter win the White House. Public payrolls are being slashed, putting the revenue of government vendors in jeopardy. But government still has to deliver services and that is creating fresh opportunities for innovative business collaborations to make government more efficient and user-friendly.

Competition is keen and only getting more so. Except for the largest and best-known companies, it take times to break into government without a track record. Companies planning to enter this market should start either by aiming lower to get some experience or by finding opportunities to be a subcontractor to an existing vendor while studying how the process works. This is not a market that can be entered or mastered without careful preparation.

Courthouses and City Halls

County governments are a good place to begin because they tend to have large budgets, diverse purchasing needs, and there is a compelling argument to be made for regionalizing functions like public safety at the county level. Budgets of some of the largest counties in the country exceed the budgets of many states. The 2011-2012 budget for Los Angeles County was set at $23.3 billion, while the state budget for Oregon was $14.7 billion.

The downside is that counties tend to be more political because many departments are headed by elected officials—tax collectors, assessors, sheriffs, justices of the peace, district attorneys, and elections officials. Each has an autonomous budget and responsibilities, and office holders always have one eye on the next election cycle.

At the municipal level, the two most common forms of government are strong mayor-council and strong city manager. In the former, the elected officials hold the purse strings and it is the city manager's job to execute their decisions. A good idea should go to the mayor or council, not the city manager's office.

Never waste a public executive's time asking for a civics lesson when there are public officials who are paid to provide information.

In a strong city manager form, the manager has budget authority and often can award sizable contracts without any input from others. The manager makes recommendations to the council and the mayor, who sign off on them.

To discover all this—in any city, county, and state agency of any size—the first call should be to the office or director of public information. Never waste a public executive's time by asking ask him or her for a civics lesson when there are public officials who are paid to provide information. Questions to ask include:

- In a city with a strong manager form, what's the threshold for awarding contracts without a bid?
- When do fiscal years start?
- When are budgets planned?
- How does one obtain a copy of the current budget?
- Do companies competing for contracts get extra points for being local businesses or for partnering with local firms?

Colleges and Universities

Universities are generally structured as strong agency entities: business decisions are made at the department level—finance, administration, facilities management, etc.—as opposed to the chancellor's or president's office.

Traditional politics is less of a factor in higher ed but many universities do give special attention to alumni and contributors. A company vying for a college's business may have an advantage if it has made significant donations, sponsored major events and projects, or counts among its executives a number of alumni.

Like all public entities, universities and community colleges maintain records

One of the faster-growing segments is community colleges. Federal funds have been funneled into programs that emphasize community development and workforce training.

that can be researched for clues about spending patterns and plans. Although state schools get a large share of their operating funds from the state, they also receive grants from the federal government and alumni donations. Public records will show how much alumni money comes in and how it's spent and what federal grants are expected and their purpose. Capital improvement budgets identify long-range plans that help vendors focus and shape their proposals. Business administration offices and CFOs drive most of the purchasing decisions.

One of the faster-growing segments is community

colleges. Enrollments have spiked as fewer students have been able to afford private school tuitions and living costs. Since the start of the Great Recession, more federal funds have been funneled into community college programs that emphasize community development and workforce training in areas such as nursing, computer sciences, and engineering trades.

Community colleges have also been spared some of the deepest cuts in higher ed budgets. New York's state legislature, for example, was going to cut all 2011-2012 higher ed budgets by 10 percent, but ended up restoring a cut of $18.2 million to community colleges.

Pennsylvania Governor Tom Corbett's proposed 2011-2012 budget slashed state support by 50 percent for four-year schools—the Penn State system, Temple, and University of Pittsburgh among them—but only trimmed community college budgets by 1 percent.

Public Schools

With school districts across the country laying off teachers and shutting down programs, the imperative is to find ways to do more with less. Almost all public schools are exploring or have adopted some form of distance learning. Districts are collaborating with other districts and other government entities to take advantage of the lower cost of shared services such as data management. Schools are looking to outsource every function they can.

Public schools receive many grants, so it helps to know about anticipated grant funding and to submit proposals before the budget is finalized, typically in late spring. Summer is often the best time to talk to business managers about future plans and expenditures. Increasingly, public schools are using cooperative purchasing programs where prevetted and preapproved vendors can sell across multiple agencies everything from technology services to flagpoles.

Small and Minority-Owned Business Quotas

For any large procurement, there is usually a subcontractor quota or goal for participation by small, local, women-owned, and minority-owned businesses. Companies hoping to win such contracts must meet or exceed the quota or risk having their carefully prepared bid eliminated on a technicality without even being read. In situations where procurement officials have to evaluate a dozen or so proposals, they tend to start by looking for reasons to disqualify some.

Most larger cities and state agencies have an office of advocacy for small and minority businesses. It should be an early stop in vetting contracting opportunities. Someone representing the company should make a personal appearance, meet the people who run the office, get on mailing lists, and attend meetings and networking events. Large contractors can recruit reliable subcontractors. Small contractors have a chance to meet prime contractors.

Questions to ask:

- How many employees can a company have and still be considered a small business? (In some locales, up to 150)
- What percentage of a procurement is usually set aside for these subcontractors?
- Is there a training program and, if so, how does it work?
- Did the government meet its small and minority business goals last year?
- Who are some of the more seasoned minority vendors?

Meet the Stakeholders

Business executives who have good ideas and solutions for decision makers can become frustrated by the slow procurement pace and cautious nature of public execs. To the untrained eye, government at times can appear arrogantly monolithic, maddeningly mysterious, or imponderably dysfunctional.

Most public servants see themselves, and expect to be treated, as professionals

It's actually a jigsaw puzzle of people, constituencies, and relationships that makes perfect sense once you get to know and work with them. As in other business ventures, most of the people working in government are conscientious and want to get it right—but not all.

In nearly every procurement there is going to be a bureaucrat involved and it helps to be able to recognize him or her to avoid unnecessary confrontations. Bureaucrats are the "Who Moved My Cheese?" folks—they tend to be inflexible, defensive, territorial, and risk averse. They see themselves as regulators whose mission is to preserve the integrity of government by rigid adherence to the rules.

The good news, however, is that most public servants are professionals and expect to be treated as such. They live in the communities they serve and they want to serve their constituencies well. The majority are interested in innovation and reform and are comfortable with a degree of risk but are cautious at all times.

Following are a few profiles of some of the key players in a typical public-private collaboration.

Purchasing Officers

Procurement—or purchasing—officers manage the contracting process, tend to operate strictly by the book, and can be quite prickly in dealing with potential bidders. Their greatest fear is inadvertently doing or saying something that will give one company an advantage over another. They tend to be so careful about being fair that they are reluctant to share even the most basic information. They are process oriented and leave the evaluation of bids to teams that are specifically responsible for reviewing and scoring proposals.

A professional and deferential approach works best, showing respect for their positions by couching questions as requests for permission: "I believe it's okay for me to ask this question, but if it is not, please tell me."

Government Attorneys

Any public-private venture involves negotiations and sign-off by government attorneys, who are also highly averse to risk. Contract terms and conditions demanded by public agencies can be hard for large companies to swallow. For example, many public contracts include a liquidated damages clause—an amount specified in advance in case of a specific contract breach.

It takes a patient corporate contract attorney to keep from scoffing at terms that, in a business-to-business transaction, might be dismissed as onerous. In my experience, I have found that it's usually a mistake to assign to government contracting negotiations an attorney who does not understand the culture of the public sector. More often that not, inexperienced attorneys will cause more problems than they solve.

It's almost always a good idea for vendors to retain a

Government attorneys have no power to strike a contract clause that is legally required, so company negotiators should not even bother asking.

designated attorney with experience in public sector contracting. Hire someone who has been in government, has negotiated from the other side, and understands that sometimes government doesn't have an option when it comes to certain terms and conditions. There is often language in contracts that's required by legislative statute and cannot be removed or altered no matter how unreasonable.

For example, in some states a multiyear procurement will contain contract language that says the contract becomes null and void should the legislature defund the agency. For any business contemplating a five-year project, that's a risky prospect, but government attorneys have no power to strike that language and corporate negotiators shouldn't bother asking. In practice, legislatures never defund agencies so it's not worth losing business over this issue.

When a large procurement is put out for bid, there is often a section that describes some of the legal terms and conditions potential vendors will be expected to agree. Many companies, upon the advice of their attorneys, make the mistake of listing all their exceptions to those terms. It's a good instinct in a business-to-business setting where, in effect, every word is negotiable. But doing so in a public-private negotiation only gives procurement officials a legitimate excuse to eliminate the bid without even reading it.

My advice to clients is to get to the negotiating table first and then be prepared to discuss under what circumstances the terms can be accepted. For example, a Request For Proposal for a software purchase may require the vendor to train the 150 people who will be using the product and to specify service or performance levels with liquidated damages in the event the vendor fails to meet them.

Instead of going into the bidding process objecting to those liquidated damages in advance, it's usually better to check the box indicating acceptance and try to work out the terms at the negotiating table. A vendor can always try to negotiate a clause, for example, that provides a sixty-day window to correct a deficiency, with liquidated damages kicking in only if the company has been grossly negligent or uncooperative.

Chief Financial Officer

In a procurement of any size, the agency's chief financial officer—sometimes titled vice president of administration—will read proposals solely to evaluate whether the bidders appear to be able to deliver on budget and on time. The CFO will look at references and especially at financial data that establishes the company's creditworthiness and stability. He or she only looks at the numbers, so it's important to provide conclusive data as part of a bid proposal.

A public sector CFO or equivalent officer will attend final negotiations to challenge a bidder's assumptions. A vendor that has submitted a proposal for outsourcing a government function promising a 20 percent reduction in costs may find the CFO wants to be convinced. The CFO must believe the numbers and the savings are real. Expect to be asked questions such as, "We know what it costs us to provide this service. Explain how you can do it for 20 percent less and still make a profit."

Chief IT Officer

The CIO will be involved if a proposal has any technology component. It is the CIO's responsibility to make sure new solutions and services will work with current systems, platforms, software, and networks. Along with the CFO and the legal department, the CIO will almost always be on the bid evaluation team.

Elected Officials

Because of ethics rules, and to avoid the appearance of favoritism, elected officials try to—and should—stay as far away from any procurement process as they can. It's rare that an elected official will sit in on meetings where agencies are considering contract proposals or interviewing bidders. They will, however, often send a staffer or a policy person with expertise in the area.

> *Successful public-private collaborations begin with establishing trust.*

That person might not speak, but he or she will be asking themselves questions of political import:

- What are the risks?
- What is the danger of failure?
- Is the vendor a good citizen in the community?
- How will the community view this decision?
- Has the company invested in the community?
- Will there be local subcontractors?
- How will this procurement play out in the press?

Later in this section I describe the tactics a potential vendor can use to anticipate these and other political questions that may arise. Successful public-private collaborations begin with establishing and building trust. Like most other aspects of doing business with government, it's more complicated than in the private sector, and it requires a more methodical approach.

The Vendor Community

The community of government contractors is an important stakeholder group from which much can be learned and gained. This is an often overlooked resource. The first step is to get to know other vendors.

The next step is to get to know as much as possible about competitors. Because government contracting requires the filing of so many public documents, it's often possible to learn revealing details about how competitors operate, what terms and conditions they agreed to in contracts they signed in the past, how they price their products or services, how they performed, and more. Later in this section I describe more specifically how to mine this information.

Vendors in related but noncompeting lines of business are a valuable source. Networking with other companies may provide a window into the prevailing culture of a public entity, who the real decision makers might be, and clues about future opportunities. Vendors with established, trusting relationships with decision makers will also sometimes influence public executives by validating or vouching for other vendors.

A telecom company can learn a lot by befriending vendors who supply data management services or computer equipment. Also, company teams that are selling into one public sector are most likely also selling to all the rest as

Vendor-community friendships are rich sources of business intelligence.

well. These vendor reps know the decision makers personally and know how the agencies tend to operate, and their knowledge can substantially shorten the learning curve. In many cases, vendors end up teaming with each other on bids.

Some jurisdictions have vendor advisory boards that include company representatives. At the federal contracting level, the President's Management Advisory Board is made up of industry and government members who review and recommend improvements in the procurement process.

A telecom company exec who has befriended a counterpart at a computer software company might ask: "What do you hear about the telecom contract? Is the agency happy with the current vendor? Have they had an audit lately? Who is on the bid evaluation team?"

These vendor-community friendships are rich sources of business intelligence.

The Public

The ultimate group of stakeholders is the public and, by proxy, the media. How to create a collaborative relationship with government's customers is discussed later.

7 Hitting the Books

T he most common complaint among government
executives is that too many aspiring vendors fail to
understand their needs and stress points and don't do
the homework ahead of time. It follows, then, that the biggest
opportunities belong to those companies that understand the
immediate needs of public officials, offer efficient solutions,
demonstrate they are going to stick around—and are prepared
to do all of this in a public arena.

Instead of marketers looking for prospects, companies
seeking business from public entities and institutions should
think of themselves as trusted advisors inventing solutions to
take to potentially compatible long-term partners. If the goal
is to turn a single transaction into an ongoing collaboration,
the first step is to gather intelligence.

Using the Freedom of Information Act

In competitive bidding for government business, the team with the most information always has an advantage. The best information comes from public records, which can usually be obtained through Freedom of Information Act (FOIA) requests.

The catalog of information that can be obtained is enormous and covers, in most states, everything from visitor sign-in sheets for the governor's office to the minutes of a municipal water authority advisory board. FOIA regulations may vary slightly from state to state but the process is usually straightforward. A Request For Information is submitted on a standard form and the materials are mailed back, usually within a specified time.

On the federal level, after a seven-year decline in the number of FOIA requests granted, the Obama administration pledged to speed up FOIA responses and to "adopt a presumption in favor of disclosure." In 2010, the administration launched FOIA.gov, a site that reports how long it takes agencies to process FOIA requests and how frequently they release the requested information versus withholding it.

On the state level, a useful resource is the National Freedom of Information Coalition at the University of Missouri (www.nfoic.org). Its website lists detailed information about each state's laws, contact information for many state agencies, and links to state FOIA advocates. In general, Florida is considered the most open with its records, and New York is considered the most protective.

In addition to budget information, companies can request bidding documents that provide a look inside proposals submitted by other contractors. Information will include values statements, differentiators, pricing structures, and capability statements. Among the most revealing documents are the agency bid evaluations. These scoring sheets show how each bidder's proposal ranked in a variety of categories.

In competitive bidding, the team with the most information has the advantage.

Where bidders scored well and where they scored poorly can reveal opportunities to compete when bid renewals come up and give a vendor a competitive advantage when competing with a company in a different state or jurisdiction.

Information gained from FOIA requests can take time, so requests should be filed early. Savvy contractors will ask for documents that include current contracts, audit reports, complaints, sanctions, etc.

FOIA requests must be very specific. Filing FOIA requests that get what you're looking for is both a science and an art. To avoid frustration and wasted time, these are best handled by specialists with experience.

Because FOIA requests are themselves publicly accessible, many contractors file them through third parties such as law firms or consultants. Companies submitting any documents to a public entity should assume that they will be discoverable by anyone. It is, however, possible to protect bid information that is proprietary by labeling it as such. In some cases, requests to seal bidding documents requires review by a state attorney general, slowing the process further.

Who's Who, What's What

Public agencies are often in the news and most issue press releases and announcements that are easily obtained on their web sites. News and announcements provide some visibility into issues, solicitations, and the backgrounds of public executives.

Another layer of information is found in public meeting agendas and minutes. Reviewing agendas can yield all sorts of valuable information about who the leaders are and which issues they care most about.

To bone up on the people behind the headlines before sitting down with them, LinkedIn.com seems to have become the preferred place where government professionals post their career details. Some maintain active Facebook pages. Public information offices usually have individual résumés as well.

Reviewing agency meeting agendas can yield all sorts of valuable information.

Government executives are often members of professional associations that are rich sources of information. Each government sector has its own professional development organizations.

Newsletters and announcements from these organizations provide insight into issues of high interest. Reviewing the agenda for the most recent National Association of City Managers' conference will reveal issues of interest to city managers. Who were their speakers? What were their topics?

All this research can be time consuming, but it is an effective precaution if it keeps a company from spending time and resources to prepare a bid for a contract it has little hope of winning. It is a wise investment if it reveals an opportunity.

The next step is preparing to meet with public executives and laying the groundwork for a trusting collaboration.

8 The Personal Touch

In a successful public-private collaboration, trust is the coin of the realm. There are many layers of trust to be earned, and the human element matters even more than it does in a business-to-business transaction, where profit is the measuring stick of success. Public officials want to do business with companies represented by individuals who:

- have studied and are conversant with the relevant issues, politics, and stakeholders;
- conduct themselves professionally and treat their public counterparts as equals;
- bring focused solutions rather than product catalogs;
- don't waste time; and
- demonstrate that their firms are committed to the public sector marketplace.

Public executives—often career public servants who have spent many years working in one agency or branch of government—put a high value on stable, lasting relationships with vendor reps. They prefer to work with people who have boned up on their jurisdictions and who will continue to be supportive after the ink has dried on the contracts.

Companies that have been the most successful in the public sector understand this dynamic and make it part of their go-to-market strategy. One of the best examples is Apple Inc.'s long courtship of public schools. Besides giving away more computer equipment than all of its competitors combined, Apple's tactics now include inviting key educators from influential school districts to the company's headquarters to meet with executives, hear lectures about how technology is changing education, and test drive new products. A report in the *New York Times* described these visits as "equal parts conversation, seminar, and backstage pass." Apple's approach yielded huge sales of its iPad for use by students who are likely to become the next generation of loyal Apple customers.

One of the more creative examples of building trust and communicating commitment is the WET In The City program (wetcity.org) created by Colorado-based MWH, one of the largest environmental engineering and construction companies in the world. MWH specializes in wet infrastructure—water systems, wastewater treatment, dams, and reservoirs.

As part of its proposals for projects, MWH offers a free, accredited educational program for school teachers on the history, science, culture, and stewardship of water ecology and use. The WET program began in 1999 and has been implemented in a number of cities, including Houston, Indianapolis, Miami, and Washington, DC.

Teachers are provided training, curriculum, and supplies for showing kids why and how to conserve water and reduce waste. MWH has an entire department within the company

Corporate charity cannot earn the level of goodwill and trust that companies enjoy when they also contribute time, treasure, and talent.

that customizes WET and other programs to suit each community, in collaboration with local organizations.

The program has been a hit with government officials who appreciate being able to provide a visible and valuable public service at no cost to taxpayers. It has the added potential benefits of reducing infrastructure costs as new generations of children grow up accustomed to wasting less water and interested in preserving natural waterways.

Government contractors routinely give back to the communities in which they operate, usually by writing checks to local charities and civic institutions. But money alone cannot earn the level of goodwill and trust that companies like MWH enjoy when they also contribute time, treasure, and talent.

Keep It Simple and Professional

One of the most common mistakes companies make is meeting with public officials without first identifying the one or two things it does well that government needs. MWH, for example, has become one of the three leading vendors of municipal wet infrastructure by targeting a specific need and establishing itself in the minds of officials as a principal provider.

Clarity matters, in every way. Public execs dislike

corporate jargon. They don't care about *verticals* or *silos*, they find alphabet soups of acronyms off-putting, and they don't have time to learn about all the great things a company might do for them. Public officials are no different from the rest of us. Tell them too much and they won't remember any of it. Presentations should be simple—we do these two or three things better than anybody else in the country.

Company reps who call on public executives should quickly establish who they are, why they are there, and what solutions they offer for current problems. Officials want to feel that a company proposing to do business with them is credible, trustworthy, has done it before, will not let a project languish, and will stay committed should a procurement run into problems.

Some firms permanently damage their chances of success with government when a high-ranking corporate executive with no experience or knowledge about interacting with public officials insists on meeting with them. If these executives ignore advice about how to conduct themselves, they risk leaving an impression of being arrogant, ignorant, or impatient. Public officials have long memories and a single bad impression can have a long-lasting effect on a vendor's ability to compete.

Unique factors in a public-private venture to remember include:

- The public customer prefers doing business with individuals who, like them, are demonstrably committed.
- The public customer lacks a profit incentive. If the transaction is a success, the reward is the personal and professional satisfaction of a job well done.
- Public officials serve demanding

constituencies that often include elected officials and other stakeholders with strong opinions, big egos, and political agendas. They are sensitive to slights, intended or not, and behavior that could be interpreted as disrespectful or unprofessional.

It's surprising how often company reps run afoul of this last point. For example, I have seen women arrive for a meeting with a public official wearing inappropriate clothing. Men will sometimes make thoughtless remarks that are instant turn-offs: "This system you're using was invented in the Stone Age."

It's also surprising how often business people forget their manners. An example I know of involved a high-ranking

It's surprising how often business people forget their manners.

corporate executive who was flown in from the home office in an East Coast city to meet with an official of an agricultural state during the final evaluation of the firm's bid for a large contract. Instead of discussing the business at hand or offering assurances of the company's stability and commitment, the executive spent too much time trying to ingratiate himself by bragging about the prize herd of pedigreed steers he kept on his trophy farm. He impressed no one and the company failed to get the award.

Becoming Visible

Vendors must do more than show up with good references and strong proposals to create confidence. Public-private ventures are intended to be long-term relationships, so it follows that they involve a fair amount of courting. There are many ways to do that with minimal effort.

In a city or county, reps should attend a few city council or county commission meetings to get a feel for the decision makers and the issues. Rather than bringing along literature to hand out or trying to initiate a substantive conversation, it's enough to shake hands and hand out business cards with a positive personal message handwritten on the back.

Being seen and showing interest in local issues leaves a strong impression on public officials. Their long, tedious public meetings are often sparsely attended, usually by people with axes to grind. A vendor looking for problems to solve is a breath of fresh air.

Smart vendor reps occasionally stop in at city hall, the county administration building, or state capital offices to leave a business card with a secretary or assistant to a public executive. "I know the boss is busy and I don't want to interrupt anything. I just wanted to stop by and say hello."

This is a surprisingly effective tactic. It tells an executive that you're around, in the community, and that you respect his or her time. It's a small gesture that sends a big message. From time to time an executive will call that rep in and initiate a conversation that could prove valuable to both parties.

When I became a Texas Railroad Commission member, it seemed as though everybody in the world wanted to get in to see me. An assistant sat outside my door to triage the onslaught. On her desk she kept a jar of candy. One of the people whose company did business with the agency would stop by periodically just to contribute some fancy candies to the jar. The genius of it is was that my assistant always gave him an appointment to see me any time he asked.

The best vendor reps were those who took the time to learn my interests and those of my executive staff. I'm an

The best vendor reps take the time to learn the interests of an agency executive and staff.

avid book reader and in my speeches I sometimes refer to those I have read on leadership. One day a vendor rep dropped off a copy of a business book with a note: "I read this and thought of you." It was a bit of a come-on, but I appreciated it.

Public execs who may not be bookworms will appreciate receiving newspaper and trade magazine clippings and printouts of online articles on relevant subjects, dropped off or mailed with personal notes. Vendor reps can also send articles about the company and about the vendor's industry that a public official might find interesting or useful. Whether or not they have already read them, it's the thought that counts. Public execs who get them will feel they have an extra set of eyes watching their backs and helping them be more successful. These are some simple ways to stay visible and build relationships.

Face Time

Establishing visibility lays the groundwork for the next step—getting a meeting and making it successful. Sometimes it begins simply by walking up to an official during a break in a public meeting or by sending an email, or both. "I know how busy you are but I wonder if you could spare just twenty minutes or designate someone who could see me. I think I have a solution to one of your current problems." It's usually more difficult.

Public execs periodically attend professional conferences where vendors exhibit and reps can meet and mingle with prospective public partners. It's not uncommon for a handful of public officials to go out for dinner and invite a vendor rep to join them. Always busy and always conscious of ethics rules, they are more likely to spend time with potential vendors at a conference than they would in their offices.

Once a meeting has been arranged, the rules of engagement continue to be keep it short and keep it simple.

Vendor reps should have their messages down pat and be able to deliver them clearly in the time allotted. If the meeting is scheduled to last twenty minutes, it should end at twenty minutes. Regardless of signals that may suggest there will be extra time, never assume that's the case. If a public exec wants more information and more time, he or she will ask. Showing respect for an official's time will be noticed, appreciated, and remembered.

Public officials generally find slide presentations tedious and off-putting. I usually counsel companies to skip them. It's better to bring printed materials. If an official is intrigued by what he or she has heard, they're going to hand those materials to a staff person to research.

> *Public officials generally find slide show presentations tedious and off-putting.*

The meeting should end with a one page leave-behind that describes the solution proposed, basic information about the company, and examples of similar projects it has completed. Every vendor should leave having asked, "What are our next steps, and who will be the follow-up contact?"

Detailed tactics and suggestions for preparing for meeting with public officials and for the meeting itself will be found in the Appendices, starting on page 169.

The Sam's Club Way

The three principal ways public-private transactions begin are competitive bidding (covered below), proposals for public-private partnerships (covered in a separate chapter), and applying for approval to be part of a cooperative buying service.

Companies whose products or services fit the model can participate in the growing area of cooperative purchasing programs which require companies go through the vetting process only once to reach a broad market. Government agencies that use the programs say they have achieved enormous savings.

Cooperative purchasing programs often offer participating agencies and nonprofits more than one vendor option for products and services. Public officials like the system because it gives them a shorter purchase timeline since they don't have to go through the full procurement process. Vendors like it for the same reason, plus it offers the benefits of economies of scale and credibility when pursuing relationships in other jurisdictions.

Coop programs vary depending on the constituency. In the education field, the K-12 market is different from the college market. Many state IT agencies have a dedicated cooperative program and it's almost impossible for a state agency to purchase from a vendor that isn't approved by the program.

Questions to ask when researching co-op programs:
- When does the coop take on new vendors: once a year, when there is demand, or can a firm apply any time?
- Which agencies/entities buy from the coop?
- How does the coop market its services?
- Which, and how many, jurisdictions are served?

To Bid, Or Not To Bid

The process of preparing a bid for a government contract is often complex and costly, with no guarantee of success. The winner of a contract may hinge on factors over which a vendor has no control. Decision makers may prefer a company whose headquarters are nearby. The vendor who currently has the contract may score lower on its evaluation but the agency or entity is unprepared or unwilling to make a switch at that time.

"There are a lot of potential clients we've preferred not to work for."

To control for these risks, successful companies turn the tables on their prospective public partners.

"We often interview a public client before deciding we want to work for them," a project manager for a large vendor company told me.

There are a lot of potential clients we've preferred not to work for because our research reveals that they don't pay their bills on a timely basis, they have a reputation for being litigious, or they tend to focus on price instead of quality. That eliminates us from bidding on some large contracts but it also helps us avoid the problems that go along with a bad fit.

A decision maker who is going to select one company over its competitors wants to feel comfortable sitting down and having a cup of coffee with the vendor's project manager. Public officials want to feel confident that if there's a problem, it's going to be addressed.

When a vendor rep asks for marketing money to pursue a bid or partnership, there is likely to be a checklist of qualifying questions that include:

The winner of a contract may hinge on factors over which a vendor has no control.

- How many times did you call on this client?
- What relationships do we have there?
- What are the project objectives?
- What is the budget?
- Does this fit with our core business?
- Who will be our competition?

Even when the answers all point to go and a company determines it has a good chance of executing a successful bid that will lead to a long-term partnership, there are times during the process when the light may turn red. It's a challenge for business people, but it sometimes happens that the plug must be pulled on a bid once it's underway, in spite of the investment of capital and pressure from the representatives who want to preserve a large commission opportunity.

Other developments that could cause a company to reconsider bidding include changes in project objectives or evaluation criteria. A vendor's bid may be undermined by a natural disaster, like a prolonged drought or a devastating hurricane, that makes it difficult or impossible for a company to fulfill its promises.

To bid or not to bid is an ongoing calculation up to the very end. It's never a go until the very last step.

Preflight Briefing

Most states and cities stage prebid vendor conferences to give potential bidders a chance to clarify the requirements and objectives. These are essential to attend. Company representatives should go early and watch the crowd. Competitors will be present and the sign-in sheet is a public document that can be obtained.

In vendor conferences, procurement officials explain the process and timeline and then solicit questions.

The instructions given at a vendor conference are specific and must be followed. A common oversight is failing to meet quotas or goals for minority, women-owned, and small-business participation.

Ingredients of Successful Proposals

The difference between success or failure often hinges on details (like quotas) that many companies overlook because the people who prepare the proposals use the wrong model. In a business-to-business transaction, almost everything is potentially negotiable. Buyer and seller are free to communicate, discuss details, throw in enhancements, and modify a Request For Proposal.

Once a public Request For Proposal has been published, officials are prohibited from communicating with vendors, except under the most formal conditions, such as written requests that are reviewed by legal departments. Proposals are scored on how well they match up with the request and whether the documents have been properly completed. A surprising number of otherwise credible companies lose business over the smallest details.

To prepare a successful proposal, it helps to know who the evaluators are and what role they play in the decision-making process. For a contract of any size, many people will be involved and each reviewer will have different objectives.

The public professionals and analysts who evaluate a proposal are usually segmented into groups. Some will only look at the solution being offered or evaluate pricing, and others will assess how well the proposal fits with existing infrastructure and programs.

Every evaluator on the team will read the executive summary and then analyze the part of the proposal that applies to their area of expertise or responsibility. Companies often make the mistake of putting their value propositions after the executive summary, which means most evaluators never see the most important part.

In order for all evaluators to read the value propositions and similar differentiators, they should be included in the executive summary and repeated in every segment of the proposal. It's the one opportunity the company has to paint the big picture in a way everyone can grasp, thus increasing the chances of winning a consensus in favor of the proposal.

Success can hinge on details many companies overlook because the people who prepare proposals are using the wrong model.

Some proposal tips gleaned from many years experience include:

- **Mention references and pricing value** in the executive summary.
- **Localize the summary.** Mention local facilities or operations that pay local taxes and employees who live in the jurisdiction.
- **Localize the look.** Include recognizable images of historic or civic significance, iconic symbols, state birds, etc.
- **Write in one voice.** Many companies assign different people to write different sections of proposals. The finished product is inconsistent. One section may be clear because it was written by someone with good writing skills, and another section might be boring because it was written by an engineer. Before a proposal is submitted, an editor should make the voice consistent.
- **Make it visual and readable.** In a culture where imagery is so important, columns of gray text cannot compete. Proposals need graphics, charts, and white space. Avoid jargon. A company with a good solution can lose if evaluators find the proposal boring or frustrating to decode.
- **Answer all questions.** Failing to answer questions, answering with only a "yes" or "no," or marking them "not applicable" usually gets a proposal eliminated. Answers should either be "no, and this is why," or "yes, and this is how." The more a company

explains itself, the better a potential public partner feels about collaborating.

- **Choose your battles wisely.** The legal requirements in a Request For Proposal often cause hand wringing in corporate law departments. This can lead to companies filing their proposals with many objections to the terms. Too many objections can get a proposal eliminated. It's usually better to avoid objections in the proposal and wait to see if the company is chosen as a finalist. Then, in the best and final stage of the process, explore with the agency or entity whether there is room to negotiate terms.

Best and Final Offers

Companies whose proposals are finalists will often be invited to submit what are known as best and final offers. Representatives are invited in to make an oral presentation to procurement officials.

Experienced government contractors craft proposals that allow for last-minute enhancements. It might be pricing but it also might be a higher level of service support or a shorter timetable for completion.

When the stakes are high, companies often have the instinct to send in an officer from corporate headquarters. This may make sense in the abstract, but in practice there is a high risk it could backfire if they haven't done their homework, can't speak to the specifics of the project, or can't connect with evaluators.

It's better to have a lower-level person make the presentation if he or she is more knowledgeable, is a better communicator, and has an established relationship with the evaluator. When corporate officers do participate at this stage, their presence should be acknowledged and they should be given the opportunity to express their appreciation for the opportunity to bid, but they should otherwise defer to the folks on the ground.

A Losing Strategy

After all the hard work and expense, in spite of having the best proposal, what happens if you lose? The moment the decision is announced, vendors should know the protest schedule and procedure, even if there is no plan to protest. The window for filing protest notices is usually less than two weeks. Protests must be specific, documented, and legitimate—a proposal was eliminated because it arrived late due to bad weather grounding air freight, for example.

A legitimate protest might be that a competitor's winning submission arrived after the deadline without a weather excuse but was accepted anyway. The stakes here are so high that bidders will often send an observer to sit in the procurement office on deadline day and watch the bids come in to make sure that all the rules have been followed.

Experienced government contractors craft proposals that allow for last-minute enhancements.

The most valuable thing a vendor can do is request an exit interview with officials in charge of the procurement. In most cases this is a formal process that public execs are required to honor. Companies that intend to compete for future business should say so and request feedback that will help them be more competitive the next time.

Once contracts are signed, losing bidders can file Freedom of Information Act requests to see all proposals that were submitted.

9 P3s, Up Close and Personal

The accelerating trend toward public-private ventures in the US is having a profound impact on the way government does business. It's being driven by economic necessity and is producing a sea change in thinking. When government runs out of downsizing options, as many have, the next logical step is to seek other funding options and privatize or outsource some of the service mandates.

P3s are not new. For decades these types of engagements have been used to build infrastructure projects, operate airports, and develop retail centers on public lands. Charter schools are essentially public-private collaborations in which a for-profit operator contracts to provide educational services in return for a stream of funding attached to each student. What is new is the sense of urgency now that public entities find themselves facing funding allocations that can no longer cover mandated services or critical needs.

In many respects, the US is late to the game. The United Kingdom has been a pioneer in P3s across a wide swath of sectors since the World War II, except they call them PFIs—private finance initiatives. The British have pioneered the P3 models that we in the US are using and reinventing today.

There are few government functions that couldn't be reinvented as collaborations between business and government. For example, there is a growing trend toward converting lotteries to P3s. Publicly funded universities have been partnering with developers to create commercial zones within their campuses that include hotels and retail stores. In exchange, the schools get new dormitories or other facilities, and the rents cover many overhead costs.

Puerto Rico's One Hundred-Schools Initiative

One of the leading jurisdictions for innovative P3s is Puerto Rico, where the government put together a massive project to overhaul one hundred aging schools in one fell swoop. Instead of contracting with many different firms, hiring designers to create plans, and then putting the work out for bid, the government has bundled everything into a single procurement. The plan called for a private developer to design and renovate or replace all of the schools over a relatively short period of time. The private sector partner will then maintain them under a decades-long services contract.

The commonwealth plans to fund the project by the traditional route of issuing bonds and will continue to operate the schools. But the government will save money based on economies of scale and private sector expertise and oversight. One vendor will do all the work, be able to source supplies for a hundred schools instead of a handful, and recruit skilled tradespeople with the promise of steady employment.

Furthermore, the contractor is more likely to build the schools well because the company will be around for decades fulfilling and getting paid for the maintenance part of the contract. Puerto Rico's school system hopes to get a state-of-the-art face lift practically overnight, and a private partner to shoulder the risk of keeping it that way.

P3s as Risk-Transfer Tools

One of the less obvious benefits of a P3 like the Puerto Rico plan is that the process requires a long-view risk analysis. In a school system, risks include fluctuations in future demand (enrollment ebbs and flows) and tax revenues. In a typical government financing of infrastructure, the risks are often obscured or glossed over and there is always a possibility that one day taxpayers find themselves on the hook for cost over-runs or revenue shortfalls. To raise the capital necessary to underwrite a P3, the private partner has to flush out all the risks and put them on the table for the scrutiny of bankers and investors.

"The transfer of risk from the public to the private sector is the most important aspect of any P3 method."

"The transfer of risk from the public to the private sector is the most unheralded, but most important, aspect of any P3 method," says Leonard Gilroy, director of government reform for the Reason Foundation.

The language of government contracting is changing to reflect the purpose of P3s. Instead of privatization, Gilroy says, "I prefer to talk about competitive sourcing, outsourcing, and partnerships. Governments have been doing P3s all along, but they haven't thought of it that way."

P3s are becoming common types of engagements between government and the private sector—from trimming trees in local parks to financing and building billion-dollar bridges. The goal of a P3 is to transfer risks and responsibilities to a private partner by dialing up or down the elements—the amount of private versus public financing, the scope of services to be provided, and how any revenue will be allocated. At its essence, trash collection is a public-private partnership in half the suburbs in the US where local governments contract for the services.

The Illinois Lottery

Governments at every level are exploring P3s, and some have championed large initiatives. For example, Illinois privatized management and operation of its state lottery a year after enabling legislation was signed into law. The lottery agency had been outsourcing bits and pieces of its operations for years, but now the state has given the private sector a much bigger management role and an incentive to grow the business.

The goal of the initiative was to generate more revenue for the state. Bids were evaluated on the basis of how much the bidder would guarantee and how likely the bidder was to deliver. The winning contender was a consortium of companies with extensive experience managing lotteries in the UK and elsewhere.

The winning consortium pledged to increase revenues to the state over the first few years by about $1 billion, and the pledge was backed up by performance bonds. Even if targets are missed, the state is guaranteed its revenue.

The state still owns the lottery and it retained control over the annual business plan. Any new games, marketing, or advertising must be approved by the state as part of the vendor's operating plan. What the vendor gets in return is the opportunity to pursue new markets and add new games to gin up the revenues. Many other states are watching and are likely to follow Illinois's example.

The P3 That Saved Central Park

Federal, state, and local parks are government-provided amenities that citizens enjoy, but their operations are often the first to get cut when budgets are tight. Public officials are finding ways to bring in the private sector to keep parks open and even turn them into revenue generators while preserving them as public assets.

On the local level, there is no fee to go for a walk in a city park. Most state parks are free as well. Local governments and some states, however, have tapped into corporate sponsorships and nonprofit community partnerships where local citizens and businesses collaborate to manage and operate public spaces and facilities.

The Central Park Conservancy was organized as a nonprofit group that became the operator.

One of the oldest and most successful park P3s is credited with rescuing New York's fabled Central Park from the dangerous and dilapidated place it was in the 1970s, when New York nearly went bankrupt. Numerous violent crimes discouraged use. The park had become a place of worn-out lawns, litter, homeless people, and criminals. There was even talk of selling some of it off to developers.

The Central Park Conservancy, through a P3, saved Central Park. It was organized by concerned citizens and business leaders as a nonprofit group that took over the park, raised funds for repairs and other projects, and effectively became the operator. It took the Conservancy many years to rehabilitate the park. Today Central Park's meadows are lush and clean, the zoo is a popular destination for tourists with children, it is the site of numerous community activities and events all week long, and it is once again a jewel in the city's crown. Revenue from fees and vendors is split with the city. Today, Central Park pays its way.

The conservancy model was later adopted for other important public spaces in New York, including the city block that is home to the iconic New York Public Library and adjoining Bryant Park. Where there once were mostly drug addicts, people now can sit and sip a latte while reading emails with free Wi-Fi. It is also the venue for major events like Fashion Week.

Many states have been aggressive about cutting park budgets. When California put seventy parks on the closure list, the legislature passed a bill to allow nonprofits to take over operation of state parks.

The federal government has long been an innovator in partnering with for-profits. For almost thirty years, the United States Forest Service has used a long-term concession model that allows private contractors to operate recreation areas and campgrounds. Vendors bear all costs and give a share of the revenue from fees and concessions to the government as payment under a long-term lease. The agency retains complete control, down to the design and color of the signs.

For almost thirty years, the US Forest Service has used a long-term concession model.

It's estimated that more than half the Forest Service recreation sites are operated by concessionaires, and some vendors have bundled contracts to operate multiple parks in a particular region.

Seven Tips for Governments and Partners

During an extended interview, Leonard Gilroy, director of government reform for Reason Foundation, listed seven things he believes government leaders should know about P3s. His observations, based on decades of study and research, are here edited.

1. No two P3s are the same.

P3s are not standardized. What works in one place may not work exactly the same in another. Each P3 engagement should be designed not according to what worked elsewhere but with a specific goal in mind. Partners should think carefully about the objective and then build a P3 to achieve it.

2. Contracts should be performance based.

Contracts should be written with outputs in mind, not based on a predetermined budget. Benchmarks and other techniques for measuring and providing penalties for underperformance and incentives for overdelivery ensure a higher level of service.

3. A P3 is like a marriage.

This is an area where P3s often run into trouble. Once a public entity signs a public-private partnership agreement, its role shifts to monitoring and evaluating performance to make sure the private partner is meeting its commitments and that taxpayers are getting what they were promised. For a P3 to be successful, government must actively monitor the agreement over the life of the contract. The public partner can never walk away.

4. P3s need expert management.

Governments with the most P3 success usually have robust pipelines of upcoming projects and dedicated centralized clearinghouses. In some cases, that means an administrative department that acts as a resource center for developing and evaluating proposals.

Governments that have had the most success with P3s have dedicated centralized clearinghouses.

Leaders in this area include the United Kingdom, some Canadian and Australian provinces, and Puerto Rico, where officials have established a separate agency: P3A Puerto Rico, short for the Puerto Rico Public-Private Partnerships Authority.

P3APuerto Rico links subject area experts to the executive branch and is responsible for helping government agencies identify needs and develop P3s; vets proposals; helps implement P3 engagements; and disseminates best practices across the commonwealth's enterprises. The goal is to ensure success and get feedback to improve the process.

Puerto Rico hired an expert consultant to help them initiate the program. Within two years of the passage of enabling legislation, Puerto Rico was remodeling one hundred schools and building a $1.5 billion toll road concession.

5. Government should solicit more input from contractors.

The bidding and competitive process provides objective feedback on critical needs. At the end of the day, public officials can always decide to keep the work in-house. The procurement process can be exploratory. Reaching out to potential partners provides real-time information that helps develop better projects. Government should not be afraid to talk to the private sector.

Instead of rushing into a formal bidding procedure, public officials can issue requests for information. Collaborations always produce better results.

> *Government should not be afraid to talk to the private sector.*

6. Build support.

The way to create consensus within a community for an innovative solution is to back up the plan with numbers. A P3 proposal should contain a financial analysis. A plan should compare a traditional model versus the P3 model. Occasionally, a P3 will cost more but when long-term value propositions are considered, it still may be better.

An infrastructure project that will initially cost more doing it as a P3 might save a great deal in maintenance over the life of the contract. And, P3 initiatives not only bring in much needed revenue, they also move the risk to the private sector.

P3A Puerto Rico does a value-for-money analysis for every project and then goes to all the local stakeholders to show and explain what they are doing.

7. Be as transparent as possible.

Government must be as transparent as possible. Otherwise, there is a danger of a public backlash. Officials should be completely transparent about the rationale for proposals and awards. For example, Puerto Rico produced and aired television commercials to explain their P3 initiatives. The message focused on economic development, better academic achievement, moving goods and services faster, and saving taxpayer revenues. The communication component was designed to help taxpayers understand the plan, and it worked.

PART FOUR

Corroborating

10 In Their Own Words
Vendors and Procurers

I nteracting as often as I do with public agency officials and private executives has given me a unique role as a cultural interpreter.

When working with the contractors, I am able to explain the way public officials think and act and why they see things as they do. That is possible because I was one of them for a decade and also because I work with them on a daily basis.

When I'm working with public officials, I can wear my entrepreneurial hat and help them find solutions for problems the private sector might be able to solve. I feel pretty wonderful when I can show executives in both the public and private sectors how collaboration is possible when it is a win-win solution for both parties.

In the process of preparing this book, I sought the input of experts and friends from both the public and the private sectors. The input I received was invaluable. Some of the interviews produced anecdotes and insights that deserve fuller exposure. What follows are excerpts from the many discussions I had with both public officials and successful government contractors. I felt the insight and advice I heard was important enough to share.

Two themes emerged: private sector contractors should work harder to build relationships and create trust, and public officials should try to be more flexible and open to innovation.

Advice from a Municipal Infrastructure Vendor

When I do business with the public sector, the most frustrated contractors I ever meet are those who either lack good people skills or simply don't take the time to develop personal relationships with public officials. It is great when one can have a casual conversation with a potential government customer without trying to get something in return at that moment. That sort of thing can be more important in doing business with government than it is in a business-to-business transaction. Relationships are built over time so it requires spending time with these customers on their home turf.

City council members and mayors often don't understand our business and don't want to.

Before you go see an official, it is great to know where they went to school, which organizations they are associated with and whether or not they have a specific problem.

For example, city council members and mayors often don't understand our business and don't want to. They are more concerned that we are visible, that our company is committed to using local subcontractors when possible, and whether or not we will move people into their community if we win a large contract.

On the staff level, they want to know us well and to be

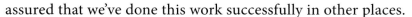

assured that we've done this work successfully in other places.

We do something we refer to as the zipper concept.

When we pursue a large contract, we map out the customer and the opportunity from top to bottom, from the mayor, city council, public works director, and selection committee, down to the equipment operator in the field. We develop a message and make sure that we have a point of contact or somebody touching every single stakeholder. We know that you simply must understand everyone's concerns.

The homework you do includes understanding the ethics rules. We are extremely careful in our dealings with any government officials or staff members because sometimes even they don't know their own procurement and state laws on what they can and cannot do.

We are also careful about how we show support in the community. We have a review board. If we want to give any community contribution or if we want to make a political contribution, it goes before our board. They check out the organization right down to the articles of incorporation and the backgrounds of the principals.

Advice from a Retired State Agency Director

The contractors I like most have people with public sector experience and knowledge. When a company decides to pursue government business, it is necessary to make a commitment to understanding the culture and the people in government.

Advice from a Public Agency Director

Not speaking the language and not knowing the rules are the most common mistakes vendors make. Just failing to understand how the government procures things and how risk averse they are about procurement is a big mistake. Pursuing public sector business requires the same sort of accountability and due diligence as any private sector business deal—sometimes more.

For example, one of the big six consulting firms was bidding for business at the agency a few years back, probably a $2-$3 million engagement. We got proposals from a number of companies—some big, some small—and there weren't any résumés in this consulting firm's proposal. They did not identify who would do the work.

They lost the bid, and then they asked for a meeting—a debrief with us about why they did not win the business. I told them that the missing résumés hurt them. They said, "Well, everybody who works with us is a high-quality professional. We didn't think it made any difference."

I said, "Then you don't know us very well. It makes a big difference to us who does the work. We want to make our own assessment about whether or not we are getting a high-quality professional. And we want to know that we are getting a professional who is experienced in working with public sector entities."

Advice from a State Agency Director

If you think government contracts are conducted in smoke-filled back rooms and are brother-in-law deals, you're more than wrong. There are some bad contracting processes, and there are some places in the country where you probably don't want to do business. But by and large, the old style politics where political friends are rewarded has been driven out of government, certainly at the state level.

The idea that if you're not politically connected you don't have a fair shot at winning government business is simply not true. We don't care who your brother-in-law is. We don't care who your friends are. We do care about your experience and your commitment to excellence. Government contracting is transparent and accountable.

If you think you can bully your way in by knowing the governor, or anybody else for that matter, think again. If you try to use that tactic, it may very well blow up in your face. That's probably the first thing I'd tell a group of private sector executives—don't try to use influence to get an advantage.

Advice from an Elected Municipal Official

What goes into a trust relationship? From a psychological perspective, first impressions matter. I've had a couple of experiences where I met someone from a vendor company and I felt, "I don't trust this person." That is unfortunate for the company, I realize, but it does impact my interest in partnering. I look for genuine, committed individuals and I usually trust my instincts about people.

I don't have a lot of time to develop relationships but that is what I look for in a private sector partner. Seventy-five percent of the success of projects can come down to relationships, commitment, and trust.

If I'm a manufacturer and I need to get bolts, I don't really care about trust. I just want to make sure that I get the bolts, that they don't break, and that the price is right. However, if we're building a multimillion-dollar infrastructure project, I have to feel good about a partner who will be working alongside me. The public scrutiny that comes with failure is extraordinary.

Advice from a Former State Agency CFO

When I was meeting with vendors, the sooner they got to a conversation as opposed to a formal presentation, the better off they were going to be. I would advise vendors to forget the formal presentations and talk to public officials about their capabilities while focusing on establishing a relationship of trust.

The other thing I would advise vendors is to keep it short. If you're scheduled for forty-five minutes, try hard to give back ten minutes of the time you were allotted. I appreciated meetings where vendors tried to give me time back. If I had more time to spare, I would tell them so. If I was in a crunch and needed the meeting to end, I was more likely to give them additional time in the future.

Advice from a Former Public IT Executive

There are a number of ways you can look at competition. There are advantages to incumbency, but incumbents can get complacent, rigid, and in a rut. Incumbents sometimes have people on the contract who have been working on the project and are resistant to change. An incumbent's margins have likely shifted since the initial contract was signed. Most incumbents will seek an increase in price on new proposals. .

This speaks to the principal challenge facing everyone seeking public business: how do you differentiate yourself? What unique value can you bring? It is important to analyze the competition and find ways to offer a better value proposition. In an age of austere budgets, the public sector has to figure out what's critical and what's not, and be flexible.

The private sector does a good job of training representatives to understand their sales pitches and know something about the products. They don't, for the most part, train reps to understand the business of their customers, which is what public officials want.

One of the trends in the private sector that translates very well to the public sector is positioning oneself as a trusted adviser. There are many ways to do that, and some of them are quite simple, such as providing a prospective public customer with intelligence that is useful to them. "You are so busy, you might not have had time to read about this but here is something that worked very well for a city about the same size as yours." "Here's an article from a trade magazine that I thought might be of interest to you."

Advice from an Infrastructure Vendor

Over the years there has been a big change in government project delivery methods. In many jurisdictions they select engineers and other project delivery professionals based on qualifications, not price. There is a price component, but it could be small, medium, or large.

Under the new alternate project delivery methods, there's more collaboration. If the client has a budget of $100 million but needs more than that will buy, both partners sit down and work together to find a solution that results in a win-win situation instead of a confrontation.

There has been a shift from about 90 percent of projects being design-bid-build, to now about 50 percent. Most of the larger projects are not hard bids, they're quality based.

Advice from a Career Public Procurement Officer

I've learned a lesson from our mistakes. Instead of asking a vendor, "Can you do this?" I now ask, "*Have* you done this?" I now ask for more specifics and I ask for references. The more a company can show that there's less risk associated with a solution, the more comfortable I am.

Advice from a Successful Vendor

A lot of times, we interview the customer before we decide to compete for the business. There are times when we feel a partnership isn't going to work.

In our firm, when someone asks for permission to pursue an opportunity, there is a checklist of questions that must be answered: How many times did you call on this client? What relationships do we have there? What are the objectives? Do they have money allocated already for the project? Is this somebody we want to work for? Is there a core stream of business?

If you score high enough on the answers, the company will grant permission and will fund the pursuit.

Advice from a Former Federal Infrastructure Executive

Public-private partnerships are always vetted well because if a business case cannot be made for the project, the dollars won't flow there. With P3s, we tend to get the infrastructure we need, not the infrastructure somebody in Washington decides that we need. That's a big win for taxpayers.

Private sector partners must think about the public policy that's being advanced by a P3. These really are partnerships. The pursuit is not for perfection but for an improvement over what we currently do. When I hear criticisms of P3s, I want to say, "Tell me where the current model does it better." P3s are the next step, not the last step in the improvement process. In time someone's going to come up with something better and different, but right now P3s are very attractive options for us.

PART FIVE

Executing

11 State Privatization Developments

The following section is a compendium of developments in privatization around the country.[1]

New Jersey Expands Privatization

New Jersey's push to lower the costs of state government through private competition began in 2010 with the creation of the New Jersey Privatization Task Force, an advisory body that issued over forty privatization recommendations.

Highway maintenance: The Department of the Treasury issued a Request For Proposals to provide privatized highway maintenance services for the Department of Transportation in a pilot program. Under the initiative, the state could hire up to three firms under a three-year contract to provide a full range of highway maintenance services—including pothole repair, landscaping, snow removal, and emergency response—in three regions of the state to compare the relative costs of public and private sector provision.

The contract was to include a variety of performance standards, including requirements that the vendor remove hazardous roadkill and debris immediately upon notification, repair potholes within forty-eight business hours, and arrive on the location of emergencies within two hours.

---

1 Material adapted with permission from Reason Foundation *2011 State Privatization Report*

State parks: The administration released a parks sustainability plan designed to improve the financial self-sufficiency of the state parks system and improve visitor services by partnering with private for-profit and nonprofit entities to expand revenue producing amenities (e.g., food, boating) in the parks. Under the plan, the New Jersey Department of Environmental Protection will continue to own, manage, and operate the parks.

In the near term, the plan aims to increase nontax resources to $15 million by 2015 through an initial round of partnerships at some of the state's largest parks. In the longer term, the plan seeks to raise about two-thirds of the annual operating budget for the park system from alternative funding sources, reducing reliance on budgeted funds. Currently, the parks system generates just $8 million in fees and concessions, or 21 percent of the total $39 million parks operating cost.

NJDEP entered into a five-year concession contract with Linx Golf Management and H&L Golf Course Maintenance Co. to take over operations and management of the 18-hole Spring Meadow Golf Course in Monmouth County. NJDEP also issued a Request For Proposals for the private management and operation of two additional state-owned, eighteen-hole public courses. NJDEP also issued a Request For Proposals for the private operation and management of food service, catering and events services at Liberty State Park in Jersey City.

State Horse Racing Facilities: To put the horse racing industry on a self-sustaining path without taxpayer and casino subsidies, officials selected private sector operators for the Meadowlands Racetrack and Monmouth Park.

Both racetracks were turned over to private sector operators that, under the terms of agreements in principle, assumed the costs to operate those facilities and took over responsibility for all simulcast wagering at the racetracks and the operation and future development of off-track wagering facilities. The New Jersey Sports and Exposition Authority (NJSEA) had previously operated the two facilities, which were losing an estimated $6-10 million per year each.

The state contracted with a developer and racetrack operator to take over operation of the Meadowlands Racetrack in a $1 per year five-year lease. Under the agreement, there will be no ongoing subsidies for purses or racing operations. The vendor plans to invest more than $90 million in a new grandstand and an off-track wagering facility.

The NJSEA selected a developer and casino owner for a five-year lease of Monmouth Park under similar terms.

Changes in state law have been necessary to facilitate the transfer. Legislation was enacted to authorize the operational takeover of horse racing from NJSEA by the private sector operators and authorizing the joint management of Monmouth Park and the Meadowlands Racetrack for a one-year transitional period.

New Jersey Lottery: New Jersey Department of the Treasury contracted with a consultant to assess the financial performance of the New Jersey Lottery and assess the desirability of privatizing its management.

Vehicle fleet ownership, operation, and maintenance: The New Jersey Department of the Treasury issued a Request For Information (RFI) soliciting private vendor responses on potential options and strategies for the ownership and maintenance of the state's Central Motor Pool and Department of Transportation passenger vehicle fleets, totaling approximately 6,500 vehicles.

Correctional food services pilot project: The New Jersey Department of the Treasury issued a Request For Proposals on behalf of the state Department of Corrections for a pilot project to provide correctional food service operations and management at Bayside State Prison and two satellite locations.

Child support payment/receipt processing: The Department of the Treasury issued a Request For Proposals on behalf of the state Department of Human Services to solicit bids on a project that would develop, implement and transition the State from a partially privatized State Disbursement Unit (SDU)—a federally mandated, centralized location for the receipt and disbursement of child support—to a fully privatized SDU. The project is intended to complement and integrate with the state's new web-based automated child support enforcement system, New Jersey Kids Deserve Support, which was designed to streamline business practices.

Montclair State University housing P3: Montclair State University completed a new residential complex that is the first public-private partnership (P3) completed under the 2010 New Jersey Economic Stimulus Act. The new $211 million complex was financed by tax-exempt bonds issued by Provident Resources Group—the owner-operator that developed, operates and maintains the complex under a long-term lease—under the auspices of the state's Economic Development Authority.

The title to the facility will transfer to the University in 40 years, unless bonds are paid off early, and until that transfer the operator is responsible for collecting rents and managing and maintaining the property in top condition. The new housing complex—which accommodates approximately 2,000 students and includes a 24,000-square-foot dining area—was built by the Alabama-based Capstone

Development Corporation and the New Jersey-based Terminal Construction Corporation.

New Jersey Transit parking: Plans to privatize parking at NJ Transit train stations failed to materialize. A NJ Transit spokeswoman was quoted as saying the delay was caused by the RFP process taking more time than anticipated. NJ Transit does not control all the parking spaces in all its train station lots, with local townships controlling about 35 percent of the spaces in most of the facilities.

NJ Transit issued a request for qualifications (RFQ) for a 30- to 50-year concession for some of its commuter parking facilities throughout the state. The proposed concession program—known as System Parking Amenity and Capacity Enhancement Strategy (SPACES)—aims to expand parking capacity and enhance services at up to three-quarters of the approximately 48,000 spaces controlled by NJ Transit statewide. The agency received statements of qualification from 10 bidder teams, which was narrowed to seven qualified concessionaires eligible to bid when the agency issues a formal Request For Proposals.

Louisiana Privatization Push

Privatization is likely to continue to play a major role in the Pelican State's streamlining efforts for the next several years.

A commission had previously identified over $1 billion in savings that could be achieved through privatization, streamlining, and consolidation. They included ongoing initiatives to outsource the administration of state employee group medical benefits and transition the state's Medicaid program into a privately delivered managed care system.

The state's streamlining efforts persuaded credit rating agencies Standard & Poor's and Fitch to upgrade the state's credit rating.

Medicaid privatization: The Louisiana Department of Health and Hospitals (DHH) selected five health care insurers to provide state-subsidized policies to over 800,000 state Medicaid patients. Under the plan, the state will transition away from its current fee-for-service model where the state pays health care providers directly for services delivered to Medicaid recipients. Instead, it will place recipients into coordinated care networks, where the state will pay the private insurers to cover Medicaid patients, and the insurers will manage patient benefits and reimburse providers for services rendered.

The new privatization program—known as Bayou Health—is designed to coordinate care among physicians, hospitals, and other health care providers to save an estimated $135 million per year out of the state's $6.7 billion Medicaid budget. At full implementation, about two-thirds of the state's 1.2 million Medicaid recipients will be served through the coordinated care networks, with approximately 400,000 recipients remaining in the current fee-for-service program.

Under the Bayou Health program, the five private networks will operate on a statewide basis under three-year contracts. Three of the networks—Amerigroup Louisiana Inc., AmeriHealth Mercy of Louisiana Inc., and Louisiana Healthcare Connections Inc.—will be paid a monthly, prepaid fee by the state for each of its Medicaid enrollees, and the firms will manage benefits, approve services, and pay providers.

Two other firms—Community Health Solutions of America Inc. and UnitedHealth of Louisiana Inc.—will operate a shared savings model, a managed fee-for-service model in which the firm shares in the savings generated by improving health outcomes and reducing costs, while continuing to pay providers on a fee-for-service basis.

Under the contracts, the amount, duration, and scope of services provided by Bayou Health insurers cannot be less than those provided under the existing state Medicaid plan.

Bayou Health faced some challenges. The process was slowed by legal challenges from several of the insurers whose bids were not selected among the five chosen by the state. All were ultimately resolved. Additionally, the state legislature enacted a bill (House Bill 207) that would have created an annual reporting requirement on program implementation and would have terminated the Medicaid privatization program at the end of 2014 if not renewed by the legislature.

Proponents suggested that the law would afford legislators the opportunity to review the program at the end of the three-year contract, but opponents countered that it was a move to undermine the administration's contracting authority. The governor ultimately vetoed the legislation.

State public employee health care PPO: The state is exploring privatization of a health insurance plan run by its Office of Group Benefits (OGB), which administers several health care plans for approximately 250,000 current and retired state employees and their dependents.

While some of OGB's health insurance plans are already operated by private firms today, the administration is exploring the potential privatization of OGB's preferred provider organization (PPO), which arranges for discounted care for over 60,000 policyholders in a network of physicians and hospitals. The administration expects that a privatization could net the state over $150 million in a one-time upfront payment.

OGB issued a Request For Proposals seeking a financial advisor to explore the potential privatization of functions related to OGB's statutory mission and provide a market valuation of the OGB's book of business. Morgan Keegan & Co. was selected over bidders Goldman Sachs and UBS Investment Bank to advise. Chaffee and Associates was chosen to establish the fair market value of OGB's operations, which was between $133 million and $217 million.

The proposal met significant pushback from state public employees and some in the legislature who fear that policyholder premiums would increase under privatization and that benefits could be reduced.

Prison sales and outsourcing: A plan to sell three prisons to generate approximately $100 million to help close a gap in state health care spending was scuttled by the House Appropriations Committee. The proposed Fiscal Year 2012 budget included a plan to privatize the operation of two prisons (Avoyelles Correctional Center and Dabadie Correctional Center) and sell three prisons (the Allen, Avoyelles, and Winn Correctional Centers) to a private operator. In addition to the expected upfront payment from the prison sales, it was estimated that the outsourced prison operations would lower the state's prison operating costs by over $200 million over the next twenty years.

The plan was immediately met with a skeptical response from public employee unions and state legislators who objected to the proposed use of one-time revenues to cover ongoing operational costs and raised other concerns related to the potential public safety impacts.

Behavioral health services: DHH selected Magellan Health Services, Inc. as the winning bidder on a contract to serve as the operator of the Statewide Management Organization (SMO) that will provide behavioral health

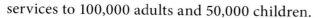

services to 100,000 adults and 50,000 children.

An executive order formally brought together the leadership of the state's four child-serving agencies—DHH, the Office of Juvenile Justice, the Department of Children and Family Services, and the Department of Education—to form a statewide, coordinated system of care for youth with significant behavioral health needs. The system is part of the Louisiana Behavioral Health Partnership, created by DHH to improve coordination of behavioral health services for all eligible children, as well as adults with serious mental illness and/or addictive disorders. The partnership covers both those in the Medicaid and uninsured populations, which will ultimately be enrolled with the SMO.

Business-charter school partnerships: A newly enacted law authorizes partnerships between Louisiana businesses and charter schools (a business-charter partnership). Under the bill, companies can receive preferred enrollment of up to 50 percent of school seats for dependents of its employees and a minority percentage of the charter school's board seats in exchange for a gift or free use of land or a facility, the major renovation of an existing facility, or a major donation of technology.

Individual businesses or groups of businesses can apply to open new schools or, in collaboration with a school district, can convert an existing school to charter status.

Ohio Privatization

JobsOhio: Legislation was signed into law creating JobsOhio, a new semiprivate, nonprofit economic development organization created by privatizing functions of the Ohio Department of Development related to the state's corporate recruitment and expansion, marketing, and job retention efforts. A plan to lease revenues from the state's liquor monopoly to JobsOhio was approved in the state's 2012-2013 budget.

Under the plan, JobsOhio will gain control of the liquor system's annual net revenues for twenty-five years in return for a $1.2 billion upfront payment funded through the sale of revenue bonds backed by liquor system profits.

According to proponents, JobsOhio's status as a private nonprofit will make it easier to conduct the state's economic development work without the bureaucratic delays and regulatory burdens seen in the public sector, making a more nimble vehicle to attract and retain businesses in Ohio.

Critics have responded that the state should have no role in picking winners and losers in the economy.

Corrections: The Ohio Department of Rehabilitation and Corrections completed a procurement that will see the state raise $72 million from the sale of one state prison to a private operator—the first sale of its kind in the nation—and two others turned over to private management, for an estimated $13 million in annualized cost savings.

Under the deal, the state will sell the Lake Erie Correctional Institution to the Corrections Corporation of America, while contracting with the new owner to continue housing state inmates there.

Management and Training Corp. (MTC) will take over operations of the North Central Correctional Institution and the currently vacant Marion Juvenile Correctional Facility. Both facilities will remain state owned. One additional facility currently operated by MTC—the North Coast Correctional Treatment Facility—will be consolidated and merged with the state-run Grafton Correctional Institution, which will remain under state operation. The state's biennial budget authorized the Department to sell up to five prisons to help close the state's budget deficit and reduce corrections costs, though the Department ultimately opted to pursue a mix of asset sales, outsourced facility operations, and facility consolidation/insourcing.

Ohio Turnpike: The Ohio Department of Transportation (ODOT)—investigating a long-term lease of the 241-mile Ohio Turnpike—selected KPMG to serve as the state's financial advisor. KPMG was to analyze various options and make recommendations on how to proceed, which could range from leaving the Turnpike in its current form, leasing it to a private operator, transferring it to ODOT or other options not yet identified.

The proposed lease allowed a term of up to seventy-five years and required solicitations and proposed business terms to be submitted to the legislature for approval before they are issued.

Ohio Lottery: The state reportedly planned to issue a Request For Proposals from consultants to analyze whether or not the state should pursue privatization of the management of the Ohio Lottery and, if so, how to best maximize its value. A provision in the 2012-2013 budget that would have authorized the privatization of lottery management was pulled in late negotiations amid legislator concerns over its constitutionality.

In other Ohio privatization news:

The 2012-2013 budget included a number of provisions granting new privatization authority to various units of state and local government. The budget authorized state higher education institutions to privatize dormitories and other facilities, while authorizing K-12 schools to privatize their transportation services. Similarly, the budget also authorized local governments and other units of government to enter into long-term leases up to thirty years in length to privatize the operations and management of their garages, meters, and other municipal parking assets.

Ohio State University trustees authorized a procurement for a potential fifty-year lease of their parking system to generate $375 million in upfront revenues, as well as avoid operational costs over the term of the agreement.

Enabling legislation became law, allowing the Ohio Department of Transportation to enter into public-private partnerships to finance, design, build, operate, and/or maintain highways, bridges, and other transportation infrastructure statewide.

The state said it was considering subleasing the operation of the Ohio Academic Resources Network—a nearly 2,000-mile fiber optic system connecting universities, schools, medical centers, and research facilities—to private businesses, according to local press reports.

State Liquor Monopolies

Washington State voters approved the privatization of the state's monopoly on the distribution and sale of distilled spirits, becoming the first state in the nation to fully shift wholesale and retail sales from public to private sector operation and potentially injecting some momentum into privatization efforts in Virginia, Pennsylvania, and other states currently exploring similar proposals.

By an overwhelming 60-40 margin, Evergreen State voters approved Initiative 1183 (I-1183), a ballot measure sponsored by Costco and other major retailers that will fully privatize both wholesale distribution and retail sales of liquor, while removing obstacles to the wholesale distribution of wine.

Among its provisions, I-1183 will dismantle the state's existing wholesale and retail monopoly by authorizing private distribution and sales of distilled spirits. I-1183 limits spirits sales to stores of over 10,000 square feet (with certain exceptions). The state expects this could increase the number of spirits retailers to 1,428, relative to 328 outlets under state operation.

With the passage of I-1183, Washington State will join thirty-two other states that have allowed private firms to distribute and sell distilled spirits since the end of prohibition. Of the eighteen remaining "control" states—a term referring to states that have a government-run monopoly on the sale and/or distribution of distilled spirits—Iowa and West Virginia privatized their spirits retail monopoly in recent decades, and Maine has more recently outsourced the operation of its wholesale monopoly to a private manager.

Pennsylvania appears to be the state best poised to potentially follow in Washington State's footsteps by privatizing its alcohol monopoly. Consulting firm Public Financial Management (PFM) conducted a valuation study for the potential privatization of the Pennsylvania Liquor Control Board's (PLCB) monopoly and found that although the current monopoly system provides the state with an average of $97 million in net revenues annually, the system's overall profitability has been on the decline as the growth in expenses has outpaced revenues.

The PFM analysis identified two viable privatization approaches:

1. Full wholesale and retail privatization, with limits around the number or types of both licenses. In the limited

retail license scenario, PFM found that about 1,500 retail licenses would be a reasonable accommodation of consumer convenience and license scarcity, and the model could be implemented through an auction process.

2. Full privatization with limited licensing of wholesale, open licensing of retail. Under the open market retail approach, PFM estimates there would likely be 3,000 to 4,000 retail licenses issued, and any qualified applicant would have an opportunity to apply for a license.

Among the key findings of the PFM report:

The limited retail license option would generate more upfront revenue. PFM estimated a valuation of retail licenses under this scenario in the range of $730 million and a valuation of wholesale licenses in the range of $575 million, for a total estimated valuation of between $1.1 billion to $1.6 billion.

The open market retail option would generate less upfront revenue but has the advantage of fewer market restrictions around retail licenses and reduced risk of suboptimal license auction results. Further, this scenario would generate more ongoing revenue from licensing, so other alcohol taxes would not need to be as high to generate the same level of alcohol revenues to the state relative to the current monopoly system.

PFM estimated that additional sales from the repatriation of sales currently lost to other states (known as border bleed) will be approximately $100 million under privatization. The Commonwealth Foundation found that bootlegging across state lines—in part driven by lower wine and spirits prices in some surrounding states—has cost the state billions in lost sales and tax revenue.

Virginia has had an ongoing policy discussion on privatizing the state's spirits monopoly. Privatization of the Commonwealth's liquor retail and wholesale operations failed to garner enough legislative support to advance, largely due to concerns that privatization would reduce alcohol-related revenues to the state.

The state hired PFM to analyze the privatization proposal, and the consultant's report found that retail license auctions would net the state an estimated $200-400 million and an additional $13 million in alcohol-related revenues on an annual basis.

Idaho: A report commissioned by Idaho's Joint Legislative Oversight Committee found that privatization of the state's liquor enterprise is feasible and outlined several potential approaches. Contracting out the operations of the thirteen state-operated stores with the lowest sales was estimated to offer $700,000 in potential annual cost savings. The administration argued that alcoholic beverage control and promoting temperance are proper functions of government under Idaho's Constitution.

North Carolina: Like Pennsylvania and Virginia, the state hired PFM to conduct a privatization analysis, which found that the state could reap approximately $300 million upfront from retail license auctions and divestiture of the wholesale operation. PFM estimated that one-time revenues could exceed $500 million if additional retail licenses and other systemic changes were approved. The issued remains one for debate.

Utah: Legislators proposed privatization after recent management scandals at the Utah Department of Alcoholic Beverage Control, as well as the agency's proposed closure of ten profitable state-run stores.

The administration expressed opposition.

Puerto Rico Privatization Program

To address the territory's chronic deficits and unsustainable debt, the commonwealth has advanced a range of reforms that include major spending reductions, optimization of government operations and the enactment of a new law inviting private investors to modernize or develop new infrastructure across a variety of sectors.

That law, Act No. 29, is now bearing fruit. It authorized government agencies to enter into public-private partnerships (P3s) with private firms for the design, construction, financing, maintenance or operation of public facilities, with a set of priority projects that include toll roads, transit, energy, water/wastewater facilities, solid waste management and ports.

The law also established a new Public-Private Partnerships Authority (P3A), a new center of excellence within the Government Development Bank for Puerto Rico responsible for identifying, evaluating, and selecting P3 projects and for monitoring and enforcing the terms of P3 contracts. The P3A has built a P3 program utilizing global best practices.

To help modernize K-12 school facilities and improve academic performance, the P3A has launched the Schools for the 21st Century P3 program, under which Puerto Rico is contracting with private operators to design, build and maintain approximately one hundred schools in municipalities. A total of forty-seven contracts were in place covering the development of seventy-six K-12 schools for an aggregate total investment of $543 million, and seventy of those schools were already under construction. The commonwealth is financing the project through the issuance of Qualified School Construction Bonds.

The P3A finalized its first major highway P3 when it reached financial close on a forty-year, $1.5 billion concession to operate the PR-22 and PR-5 toll roads. The agency prequalified potential bidders and ended up with two firm bids. The winner was Autopistas Metropolitanas de Puerto Rico, LLC—a consortium of Goldman Sachs Infrastructure Partners II (an infrastructure investment fund) and Abertis Infraestructuras (a Spanish toll concession company). The consortium will pay the commonwealth an upfront payment of $1.136 billion, will invest $56 million in initial safety upgrades, and will invest an estimated $300 million in highway maintenance over the life of the concession.

Under the terms of the contract, the concessionaire may not increase tolls until 2014, after which any future increases will require government approval.

P3A officials advances privatization of San Juan's Luis Muñoz Marin International Airport, the busiest airport in the Caribbean. The airport's leading carrier, American Airlines, agreed to the terms of a draft concession agreement, with other airlines following suit.

The P3A and the Puerto Rico Ports Authority issued a request for qualifications that yielded twelve responses from potential bidders. The Authority's shortlist of six consortia eligible to bid on the project, included teams led by ASUR, Fraport, GMR, and Zurich Airport. Bids were to have been submitted by the end of the year for a 50-year lease.

The Authority's board of directors directed staff to begin an evaluation process and develop feasibility studies for several potential projects, including a new minimum custody correctional facility, a ferry between the municipality of Fajardo and the municipalities of Vieques and Culebra, a technology project for traffic control automation and traffic violation control and redevelopment initiative targeting areas surrounding Tren Urbano (San Juan's regional rapid transit system) stations.

Arizona Commission Privatization Review

Arizona's Commission on Privatization and Efficiency (COPE) issued the second of two reports outlining a set of privatization and government efficiency recommendations to streamline the state and deliver more cost-effective services to taxpayers.

Key recommendations included:

- Designing a sound privatization process to ensure that any future contracting efforts be done with proper due diligence and adherence to best practices: Specifically, COPE discussed recommending the creation of a privatization center of excellence to establish a standardized privatization process, conduct business cases of proposed privatization initiatives, monitor project implementation and disseminate best practices, among other tasks.

- Privatizing operation and management of the Arizona Lottery: COPE recommended that the state explore the potential private sector operation and management of the Arizona Lottery as a means to increase state lottery revenues by an estimated $107-210 million over a five-year period. COPE found that the Arizona Lottery has been an underperforming asset, with costs rising faster than revenues in recent years. COPE cited a similar privatization in Illinois—where a private operator has committed to increasing the state's lottery proceeds by over $1 billion in a ten-year contract.

- Expanding public-private partnerships (P3s) for state park operation: COPE recommended the expanded use of P3s for the operation and management of entire parks throughout the state parks system to ensure that parks remain open and properly maintained, as well as to take significant costs off the state's books.
- Implementing an activity-based costing pilot program: Noting its inability to acquire reliable information on the internal costs of operation for a variety of commonly- outsourced administrative support services, COPE recommended that the legislature adopt a statute setting forth an activity-based costing pilot program. It would assess the full costs and potential efficiency/privatization opportunities in several service areas, including vehicle fleet operations, maintenance and management; printing and document management; building/facility operations and maintenance; and mail services.
- State agency review process: COPE outlined a recommended framework for a systematic review of agencies, boards and commissions for potential elimination, merger, efficiency review and/or privatization opportunities. COPE's recommended process would include the systematic review of 20 percent of the state's agencies, boards and commissions each year on a five-year rotating basis.
- Adopt statewide outcome-based budgeting: COPE recommended that Arizona policymakers shift to an outcome-based budgeting process that integrates the concepts of zero-based and performance-based budgeting. Washington State, Iowa and others have used a similar approach, whereby policy makers and the public collaboratively rank programs according to

their performance and costeffectiveness and the state funds down the list with available revenues to ensure that the highest priority and highest performing programs are funded first.

The two COPE reports detailed a number of additional privatization and efficiency recommendations across a broad range of government services and systems, including:

- Public employee pension reform;
- State personnel reform;
- State procurement reform;
- Statewide student-based budgeting;
- Privatization of environmental permit processing;
- Privatization of highway rest areas;
- Privatization of building maintenance;
- Privatization of education data collection;
- Consolidation of email systems;
- Shared services in human resources;
- Improved real property management;
- Improved cell phone contract management;
- Improved personal computer power management;
- Expansion of electronic tax filing and reduction of revenue offices; and
- Interdepartmental exchange of surplus equipment.

The Arizona Senate passed legislation in 2011 requiring the director of the Arizona Department of Transportation (ADOT) to authorize third parties to perform all title and registration, motor carrier licensing, and tax reporting, dealer licensing and driver license functions. The House of Representatives amended the bill to remove the privatization mandate, replacing it with language requiring ADOT to submit a report to the governor and legislature by the end of the year that reviews the agency's current provision of services by third parties and offers recommendations on expanding

the privatization of ADOT services. The Senate later approved the House's changes, and the governor signed the bill into law.

Texas and Connecticut Infrastructure P3 Laws

Over the last decade, **Texas** has been a pioneer in using private sector financing and project delivery to deploy new transportation infrastructure through public-private partnerships (P3s). The Texas legislature re-embraced transportation P3s for roughly a dozen new transportation projects through 2015. Simultaneously, the legislature also enacted Senate Bill 1048 (SB 1048), significantly expanding the Lone Star State's ability to tap infrastructure P3s for more than just transportation projects. Texas can now use P3s to deliver nearly any type of public infrastructure, including schools, water and wastewater projects, transit, ports, and other public use facilities.

Modeled after Virginia's Public-Private Educational Facilities Infrastructure Act—which has been used extensively by agencies in the Commonwealth to deliver a wide range of projects since its enactment in 2002—SB 1048 allows for both solicited and unsolicited proposals from private firms to develop infrastructure projects across a broad spectrum.

Under SB 1048, qualifying P3 projects include, but are not limited to, "any ferry, mass transit facility, vehicle parking facility, port facility, power generation facility, fuel supply facility, oil or gas pipeline, water supply facility, public work, waste treatment facility, hospital, school, medical or nursing care facility, recreational facility, public building, or other similar facility currently available or to be made available to a governmental entity for public use."

The law establishes the Texas Partnership Advisory Commission to provide legislative review and oversight

The Texas Facilities Commission adopted new guidelines to govern the P3 process, which is seen as an important tool for further developing the Capitol complex in Austin and reducing the state's use of leased office space.

Connecticut became the second state to authorize P3s across a broad range of sectors, with statutory authority for P3s included as part of a larger jobs and growth bill. The law authorized state executive branch agencies to enter into P3 agreements to finance, design, construct, develop, operate, and/or maintain state facilities that include: educational, health, early childcare, or housing facilities; transportation systems, including ports, transit-oriented development, and related infrastructure; and any other facility the legislature identifies or proposes as a project.

The bill is more limited in scope than Texas', limiting the total number of P3 projects to five, which must be in place before P3 authority expires on January 1, 2015. The bill authorizes the blending of public and private funds to finance P3 projects, though state support cannot exceed 25 percent of the project's cost. P3 contracts are limited to a maximum of fifty years in length and may include the collection of user fees, except that any proposed highway tolls would require prior legislative approval.

The bill creates several layers of P3 oversight. Projects must approved by the governor, heard in public hearings by several legislative committees, and reviewed by the state's contracting standards board. Approved projects must be competitively solicited, and the process requires the preparation of a value-for-money analysis to assess whether a P3 procurement offers the best value to the state relative to alternative delivery methods. Further, private sector partners on completed projects will be required to submit annual independent audit reports to its public sector partner agencies.

Concessions in the bill language were made at the behest of public employee unions, including requirements that subject P3s to the state's prevailing wage laws (or labor wage rates established in project labor agreements) and carve out a potential, ongoing operational role for public employees in some P3 projects.

"Yellow Pages Test" in Pennsylvania

In addition to exploring the potential privatization of the Pennsylvania Liquor Control Board's monopoly, the administration directed state agencies to plan for reduced operating funds in the 2012-2013 cycle and to propose opportunities for outsourcing, privatization, public-private partnerships, or competition to lower costs. According to the administrative circular, "Agencies should identify opportunities for functional outsourcing or consolidations. The 'Yellow Pages' test provides a good place to start. If a product or service that state government is currently providing can be found in the Yellow Pages and can be done less expensively by the private sector, then the commonwealth should consider offering that product or service in a different manner."

A Governor's Advisory Council on Privatization and Innovation was formed to review government functions and services to determine whether the state is providing the most cost-efficient and transparent government and whether any in-house government functions might be better and more cost effectively performed by the private sector.

Bloomberg BusinessWeek reported that the administration had hired investment bank Greenhill & Co. to undertake a review of all state assets and services (with the exception of the state's liquor monopoly) to identify potential privatization and asset divestiture opportunities.

The administration indicated its opposition to any long-term lease of the Pennsylvania Turnpike and the privatization of public prison operations.

Washington State Privatization Moves

Executive Order 10-07 required agencies to use performance-based contracts when contracting for state services and directed the state's Office of Financial Management (OFM) to develop minimum performance contracting standards for client and personal services contracts. The State Auditor's Office issued a report finding that agencies were in "various stages of transition to performance-based contracting":

- Over 90 percent of state contracts reviewed met OFM's basic performance-based contracting standard by identifying deliverables and tying vendor payment to successful completion or delivery.
- About 50 percent of contracts identified performance measures or outcomes.

The report suggested that the state "create a centralized office or staff with a high degree of expertise in performance measurement and performance-based contracting to provide technical assistance to agencies in developing and improving their use of performance measures and outcomes."

Several administrative agencies and activities—including state printing, motor pool, mail services and information technology—are being consolidated into two new agencies: the Department of Enterprise Services and the Department of Consolidated Technology Services. The restructuring is expected to save at least $18 million and eliminate up to 115 state information services employees.

The State Auditor's Office released a performance audit that found that the state's print services were not a core function of government and recommended that the Department of Printing be required to compete against private printers for all printing work.

State Parks Privatization on the Rise

Policy makers in several states—**Arizona** and **Utah**, most notably—explored the expanded use of privatization in the operation of state parks as a means to keep parks open.

The privatization model most discussed—one used extensively by the US Forest Service (USFS) for over twenty-five years—is a method of P3 in which a state enters into a lease (concession) authorizing the operation of one or more parks by a private recreation management company (concessionaire) under a performance-based contract.

Under a parks operation P3, a concessionaire takes most or all of a park's operations and maintenance costs off the state's books and retains the revenues collected from entrance, camping, and other user fees, in return paying the state an annual lease payment based on a percentage of the fees collected (typically 5-15 percent of gross revenues). The state retains full ownership of the land, and the company is subject to strict state controls on operations, visitor fees, maintenance and other key issues.

This P3 model would expand the scope of private operation in state parks beyond the ubiquitous concessions used by many states in which a private company runs a retail store, food, lodging, or equipment rental operation within a government park. For example, private concessionaires currently operate the commercial activities (e.g., lodging, retail, food) in the crown jewels of the national parks, including the Grand Canyon, Yosemite, and Yellowstone.

However, this is a more limited type of concession than discussed above. Agencies such as the USFS, Tennessee Valley Authority, and Lower Colorado River Authority have made extensive use of concessionaires to operate and maintain complete parks and campgrounds under park operations P3s. In fact, the USFS has been consistently and successfully applying this model for over twenty-five years throughout many parts of its system.

In **Arizona**, policy makers explored alternative management options designed to lower costs and create a self-sufficient parks system. While Arizona State Parks (ASP) has entered into a range of partnerships with local governments and Native American tribes to keep several parks open, these partnerships are of a short-term nature and do not ensure the long-term viability of the parks, leading to calls to explore the potential for parks operation P3s.

The Arizona State Parks Foundation issued a report evaluating ways in which the state could pursue more partnerships with private entities and introduce systemic efficiencies to lead the state parks system towards financial sustainability. The report found that "[t]here are certain functions of the Arizona State Park System, as well as potential new opportunities, that are better suited for the private sector or other public providers to either manage or pursue, or to share the responsibilities with state parks."

Services identified as most ripe for privatization within the state park system included asset management and maintenance, accommodations, food, hospitality, retail, and recreational services.

Utah: A performance audit of the state parks system issued by the Utah's legislative auditor general recommended that the state's Division of Parks and Recreation adopt a more businesslike operation to improve park system efficiency and recommended the adoption of a pilot program to evaluate the effectiveness of parks operation P3s. The audit noted that,

> "the best example of full operational privatization is the USFS. Officials from the USFS report it is a common practice in federal forests to allow private businesses to manage forest campgrounds and marinas, as well as offer additional concession services through the issuance of permits. The USFS typically issues five-year concession permits with a possible five-year extension based on performance; however, they also consider a longer-term permit if concessionaires will utilize their own capital goods on forestry land. Typically, the USFS retains responsibility for capital projects, unless special terms are negotiated, and retains the right to revoke a concession permit at any time. The local county sheriff typically provides law enforcement."

The Utah Privatization Policy Board rejected any outright sales of state parks.

California: The administration announced plans to shutter seventy of the state's 278 state parks in response to the state's fiscal challenges. The proposed prompted passage of legislation granting the state Department of Parks and

Recreation the authority to enter into P3s with nonprofit organizations to take over the operations of state parks threatened with closure.

Florida: Florida's Acquisition and Restoration Council approved a state Department of Environmental Protection plan to accelerate a proposed P3 initiative that would expand camping and RV facilities at fifty-six state parks. The new camping/RV facilities would be financed, built, and operated by private entities, with the agency retaining full control over all aspects of planning, design, construction and operation.

The agency uses nearly a hundred private-sector partners to operate various concessions within the state parks system. Recreation service provider Cape Leisure Corp. took over various concession operations at three state parks

Hawaii: Legislation was enacted to transfer state-owned lands to a new Public Land Development Corporation, a development arm of the state's Department of Land and Natural Resources. It was authorized to form P3s to develop state land, renovate public recreation and leisure assets, and generate revenues to offset major departmental budget cuts in recent years. The corporation can also issue revenue bonds for land acquisition and the construction or renovation of state facilities.

New Jersey: A parks sustainability plan prepared by the administration aims to increase nontax resources to $15 million by 2015 through an initial round of partnerships at some of the state's largest parks. In the longer term, the plan seeks to raise about two-thirds of the annual operating budget for the park system from alternative funding sources. Currently, the parks system generates just $8 million in fees and concessions, or 21 percent of the total $39 million parks operating cost.

The New Jersey Department of Environmental Protection

(NJDEP) announced a five-year concession contract with Linx Golf Management and H&L Golf Course Maintenance Co. to operate and manage a golf course in Monmouth County. The consortium will pay the state an annual $130,000 fee (with 3 percent increases each year), as well as 15 percent of total gross revenues in excess of $1 million annually. Several other golf courses were being considered for similar P3s.

NJDEP issued a Request For Proposals for the private operation and management of food service, catering and events services at Liberty State Park in Jersey City. The winning bidder will pay the state a fixed annual fee plus a percentage of the annual gross revenue earned from park operations.

New York: The New York State Office of Parks, Recreation and Historic Preservation (OPRHP) entered into a five-year concession contract with CLAW Golf Management to operate the Springbrook Greens State Golf Course and a separate five-year concession with CDK Golf Enterprises to operate the Pinnacle State Golf Course. Under both concessions, the private operator will assume all aspects of golf course operation—including revenue collection, turf management, food sales, retail sales and cart rentals—and will cover all associated operating costs, including staff, utilities, and insurance.

Oklahoma: An Oklahoma legislative committee launched an interim study on state parks privatization. The Department of Tourism and Recreation said full privatization of state parks was unfeasible due to federal restrictions that prevent removal of lands from the state park system that were originally acquired using federal conservation funds.

States Explore Private Lottery Management

Illinois: A private consortium took over operations of the Illinois Lottery, formally launching a first-of-its-kind lottery privatization initiative. Officials expect the move to generate $4.8 billion for the state over the next five years, a $1.1 billion increase over the revenues projected under state management. Under the terms of the ten-year contract, the winning bidder—Northstar Lottery Group, a partnership between GTECH, Scientific Games, and Energy BBDO—will take over responsibility for lottery operations, management, and marketing functions in exchange for a portion of revenues. The state will continue to exercise control and oversight over all significant business decisions, including the state approval of annual business plans and the ability to access all vendor information regarding lottery operations.

The deal also ties the operator's compensation to its performance at enhancing lottery revenues. Through a combination of an annual $15 million management fee and incentives for extra profits, Northstar stands to earn over $330 million over five years if it reaches state-determined revenue targets. However, the contract includes a 5 percent total net income cap on the potential profits for the contractor, as well as penalties paid to the state if the company fails to hit revenue targets. The contractor will retain all current lottery employees and has announced its intention to hire an additional one hundred private sector employees.

Under the privatization initiative, enhanced lottery revenues will be earmarked for education funding and new capital projects included in an infrastructure program approved by the legislature in 2009. Northstar's strategy to increase revenues involves a combination of attracting more players, expanding the product line, and adding hundreds of new outlets for lottery ticket purchases across the state. A June 2011 article in the *State Journal-Register* noted that Northstar is making progress on several of these fronts.

Arizona: The Commission on Privatization and Efficiency recommended that the state explore the potential private sector operation and management of the Arizona Lottery. COPE's analysis found that the Arizona Lottery has been an underperforming asset that potentially increases revenues by an estimated $107-210 million under a system similar to the one in Illinois.

California: The Camelot Group—which operates the national lottery in the United Kingdom and advises California's lottery—reportedly has had preliminary conversations regarding a lottery privatization proposal with state officials and public employee groups. Any move to privatize lottery management would require legislative approval and would be subject to competitive bidding.

Missouri: The State Senate's Rebooting Government working group—designed to develop a package of streamlining and cost-saving reforms—issued a set of recommendations that included privatization of the Missouri Lottery.

New Jersey: The Department of the Treasury contracted with a consultant to assess the financial performance of the New Jersey Lottery and assess the desirability of privatizing its management.

Ohio: State legislators removed a provision in the 2012-2013 budget before passage that would have authorized the privatization of the management of the Ohio Lottery. The administration announced plans to issue a Request For Proposals from consultants to analyze the potential for privatized lottery management.

Washington State: The administration requested lottery

officials issue an RFP for a study to analyze privatization the state's lottery.

Indiana Welfare Eligibility Privatization Program

Indiana's privatized welfare eligibility modernization program received federal authorization to expand throughout the state.

The state had launched a ten-year, $1.34 billion contract to automate eligibility determinations for food stamps, Medicaid, and other welfare benefits and significantly reduce face-to-face meeting requirements via more computerized processes. However, the system was overwhelmed with a recession-related spike in applications and widespread complaints from people who lost their food stamps or Medicaid coverage or who had difficulty utilizing new call centers or the new online application for welfare benefits.

This led the state to pursue a revamped hybrid approach that relies more on face-to-face contact while enhancing some of the previous technological improvements. The state contracted for the services of Xerox subsidiary Affiliated Computer Services (ACS)—IBM's primary subcontractor on the original privatization—in an eight-year, $638 million service contract. According to administration officials:

- Client inquiries are down 40 percent.
- Caseload backlogs have been reduced by 79 percent.
- Call abandonment rates remain below 5 percent.
- The current timeliness rate for food stamp application processing is 95.97 percent.

- Positive and negative error rates remain below the national average.

The Indiana Family and Social Services Administration (FSSA) received a federal award of $1.6 million in recognition of its progress in reducing food stamp error rates.

Higher Education P3s

State university systems are exploring innovative service and asset delivery models to help reduce costs, better maintain facilities, and create new ways to build and modernize their assets. Some systems and schools have turned to the private sector to achieve these goals in various ways, ranging from the outsourcing of specific operational services to P3s that bring private sector capital and expertise to bear on the financing of university facilities.

Arizona: The University of Arizona selected Capstone Development Corp. and Peach Properties, to develop two new student apartment housing facilities under P3s. Capstone will develop Plazo Centro, a mixed-use, 720-bed student apartment housing facility to be located along the new streetcar line in downtown Tucson. The plan also includes a parking garage and more than 25,000 square feet of commercial space. Similarly, Peach Properties will develop a 320-bed apartment complex along the streetcar line that includes 18,000 square feet of commercial space.

Florida: Officials at Florida Atlantic University (FAU) opened the Innovation Village Apartments, a 1,216-bed student residential and mixed use project on the Boca Raton campus developed under a $123 million P3 with Balfour Beatty Campus Solutions, LLC and Capstone Companies.

Accelerated construction on the $123 million project began in March 2010 and was delivered on schedule for the start of the 2011-2012 academic year.

Under the P3, the private partner developed the new facility and will comanage both it and the other existing student housing facilities on the Boca Raton campus in tandem with the university. The project was financed through a combination of tax-exempt bonds and Build America Bonds issued by the FAU Finance Corporation, and partner Balfour Beatty invested in the project by purchasing $3.4 million of tax-exempt bonds.

Kansas: The state legislature directed the Kansas Board of Regents to explore the potential outsourcing of university functions like dormitory operations and custodial services to private vendors.

Louisiana: RICOH took over operations of university mail and copying services at Louisiana State University in an initiative officials expect will eliminate an annual operating subsidy for these services of over $400,000. The company has renovated the ground floor of the LSU Student Union, creating a central location for students to receive mail, copying, and other related services. The ten-year contract sets maximum rates that RICOH can charge students for mailboxes and gives the university approval over postal rates charged to customers.

Missouri: The University of Missouri hired a brokerage firm to analyze the potential privatization of the university's animal research laboratory. The firm reportedly will help the university identify potential buyers and financing options for the facility and estimate its market value. The Research Animal Diagnostic Laboratory has been at the university for more than forty years and serves companies that care for and use animals in biomedical research, also providing biological and genetic testing services.

New Jersey: Montclair State University completed The Heights, a new residential complex that is the first P3 completed under the 2010 New Jersey Economic Stimulus Act. The new $211 million complex was financed by tax-exempt bonds issued by Provident Resources Group—the owner-operator that developed, operates, and maintains the complex under a long-term lease—under the auspices of the state's Economic Development Authority.

The title to the facility will transfer to the University in forty years, unless bonds are paid off early, and until that transfer the operator is responsible for collecting rents and managing and maintaining the property in top condition. The new housing complex—which accommodates approximately 2,000 students and includes a 24,000-square-foot dining area—was built by the Alabama-based Capstone Development Corporation and the New Jersey-based Terminal Construction Corporation.

Ohio: Ohio State University (OSU) qualified seven of ten consortia submitting responses to a request for qualifications for a potential long-term lease for the operations and maintenance of its parking assets. The university is seeking to lease over 35,000 parking spaces to a private operator in return for a minimum $375 million upfront payment under a concession not to exceed fifty years.

OSU's parking initiative is the first project advanced as part of a larger, comprehensive review of all of its noncore assets to see how they could be leveraged to generate additional revenue to support the university's academic mission. The university said it is reviewing the Don Scott Airport, the university's golf courses, and other large tracts of land not necessary to the core academic mission to determine if leasing or selling them could benefit the school's

core mission. The list of potential assets for full or partial divestiture will not include housing.

Privatization and Child Welfare Reform

Flexible child welfare funding, where the money follows the needs of the child rather than the service provider, has allowed states to innovate and is a key component in the successful implementation of privatization and child welfare reform. In September 2011 Congress passed and President Obama signed the Child and Family Services Improvement and Innovation Act. This new child-welfare law creates a foster care financing framework that more readily supports child welfare reform and privatization efforts. Passage of this law means that states will be better able to invest in initiatives that help improve child safety and family stability as well as move children from foster care into safe permanent homes.

The new law renews child welfare waiver authority to allow more states to invest in new ways of serving children at risk of abuse and neglect. The Department of Health and Human Services can now grant up to ten new state waivers per year through fiscal year 2014. These renewable waivers last for five years, allow states to be innovative, and let them have more flexibility in the use of federal foster care dollars. In addition, the law establishes a process to create uniform child welfare data standards that can help drive further improvement to the foster care system.

Existing waivers in places Ohio, Illinois, and Florida have helped prevent child abuse and neglect, helped more children remain safely in their own homes, and improved the quality of services to vulnerable children and families.

Highway Rest Area Partnerships

Though federal law prevents most states from fully privatizing the operation of highway rest areas, Virginia and Georgia both advanced initiatives to significantly increase the scope for private sector funding and operation.

In Virginia, the administration awarded a three-year contract to CRH Catering Co., Inc. to develop and manage a new program to expand traveler services at the state's forty-two safety rest areas and welcome centers, using new revenues generated through sponsorships, vending, and advertising to offset rest area operating costs.

CRH will pay the Virginia Department of Transportation (VDOT) a guaranteed annual fee of approximately $2 million—nearly $300,000 more per year than VDOT previously received from vending and advertising—to help offset costs for operating the rest areas, in addition to annual revenue-sharing payments based on a percentage of sales generated from sponsorship, advertising, and vending operations. The private manager will oversee the installation of new advertising and vending machines at rest areas with more consumer choices for food, beverages, and merchandise, as well as new ATM machines and interactive kiosks at welcome centers offering information on Virginia's top attractions and travel destinations.

In Georgia, state transportation officials shortlisted two private bidders in a similar procurement to advance the state's Rest Area and Welcome Center Management Program, which aims to sell or lease of advertising space and sponsorships at seventeen safety rest areas and nine welcome centers along the interstate system in Georgia to fully fund the cost of maintenance and operations of those facilities.

The two bidding teams—DBi Services/The InterConnect Group and Infrastructure Corporation of America/Travelers Marketing—will compete to develop, implement, and manage an advertising and sponsorship program and serve as a turnkey operator to manage facility operations and maintenance.

Connecticut has entered into a thirty-five-year public-private partnership (P3) with the Carlyle Group to refurbish and operate the state's twenty-three highway service plazas in return for a state share of revenues raised. Under the deal, the Carlyle Group will invest $178 million in the state's rest areas and will attract new restaurants and businesses to the facilities.

Other State Privatization News

California: Legislation was enacted that would require state agencies to immediately cancel service contracts with private vendors if the State Personnel Board deems those contracts to be in violation of state law. It prohibits agencies from entering into another contract for the same or similar services or to continue the services that were the subject of the cancelled contract.

Colorado: Legislation was enacted creating a new process to expedite air quality permitting in the Colorado Department of Public Health and Environment by allowing the agency to prequalify and use private sector modeling contractors. Applicants seeking permits can use the preapproved third-party modeling firms to accelerate the permitting process if the applicant agrees to cover both the contractor's and the state's costs. According to a Joint Budget Committee analysis of the bill, the state receives up to 3,000 air permit applications annually, but it faced a backlog of about 1,200 unprocessed air permit applications in 2011 alone, predominantly from the oil and gas industry.

The administration ordered a review of a restructuring proposal from Pinnacol Assurance—the state-owned insurer that provides over half of the workers' compensation insurance policies in the state—that would transform it into a private mutual insurance company.

Under Pinnacol's proposal, the insurer would convert itself into a privately held mutual assurance company, granting the state a $340 million, 40 percent ownership stake that would generate $13.6 million in annual dividends potentially split between education and economic development. The company would remain based in Colorado but would be able to expand its business into other states.

A nineteen-member stakeholder task force was appointed to review the proposal.

Florida: New legislation was enacted that authorizes a P3 that will privatize nearly all correctional facilities and services in South Florida and require a range of over forty performance measures that include reducing recidivism, expanding offender treatment and programming, and achieving other key rehabilitation and safety goals. Privatization will not proceed unless the state realizes savings of at least 7 percent, as required under state law.

Key to achieving the equal goals of spending reduction and improved performance in rehabilitation is the structure of the privatization initiative, which bundles up the bulk of correctional services in a large geographic area under one contract. Florida's proposed P3 applies a continuum of care approach that coordinates and links evaluations, programs, and resources for inmates across facilities and levels of care.

According to proponents, spending a lot of resources on uneven, uncoordinated programming for an inmate across various facilities and levels of care delivers a poor return on expenditures, and coordination across a continuum of care would maximize the value of every tax dollar spent.

Florida's privatization initiative will be the first attempt to create a continuum of care in corrections. The procurement was placed on a temporary hold pending resolution of multiple lawsuits filed by public employee unions representing state prison guards.

New legislation enacted expands a five-county Medicaid privatization pilot program statewide, creating a fully integrated managed care system for nearly three million Medicaid recipients for all covered services, including primary and acute care and long-term residential or community-based care. Medicaid spending costs Florida $20 billion a year.

The new law establishes a statewide managed care program, under which qualified managed care plans will compete to provide services under a set of strict selection criteria. The program will be broken down along regional lines, with the state selecting a limited number of competing plans in each of eleven regions to ensure coverage in rural areas.

Participation is mandatory for most patient populations, though the law includes an opt-out program to allow Medicaid recipients to use their state subsidies to purchase other forms of health care coverage.

The Florida Government Efficiency Task Force issued recommendations that included streamlining the state procurement process; creating a real property database to help assess asset divestiture opportunities; and privatizing a range of assets and services that include state insurer Citizens Property Insurance Corporation, public sector toll roads, ports, and correctional facilities. The advisory body meets every four years.

Citizens, the largest state insurer at 1.4 million policies, has been generating insufficient revenues to cover large-scale hurricane losses, leaving taxpayers at risk. Citizens has 1.4 million customers, and a premium revenue stream of close to $3 billion a year.

Georgia: The Georgia Department of Transportation (GDOT) initiated a major highway maintenance privatization project, awarding a three-year, $6.8 million contract to Roy Jorgensen Associates to maintain the state's stretch of Interstate 95, which was recently widened in a $1 billion expansion project. The contract is Georgia's first performance-based highway maintenance project, with the contractor responsible for all normal maintenance activities along Georgia's entire portion of Interstate 95. This includes litter and roadway debris removal, mowing, guardrail repair, routine bridge repair, pothole repair, tree trimming, maintenance of drainage features, signage, traffic control devices, emergency incident response, and clearance assistance. The contract also covers all related ramps, frontage roads, bridges, and roadway appurtenances.

The Georgia Department of Audits and Accounts released a performance audit of contracts the Department of Community Health (DCH) holds with three private care management organizations (CMOs) to administer health care programs for approximately 1.1 million low-income individuals in the state's Medicaid and PeachCare for Kids programs.

The audit found that the programs were successful at keeping health care cost escalation in check. Collectively, the CMOs were paid approximately $2.7 billion in fiscal year 2010, an increase of about $400 million in two years primarily due to membership growth. Per-patient payments rose from $203.15 per month in Fiscal Year 2008 to $206.02 in Fiscal Year 2010, an increase of 1.4 percent, significantly lower than premium escalation in the larger private health care market.

The audit also found that the CMOs had relatively small or negative profit margins in calendar year 2009, with none exceeding 1.6 percent. CMOs also spent more than 85 percent of revenue on members' health care benefits in 2008 and 2009, consistent with industry best practices. According to surveys conducted for two CMOs, the percentage of providers satisfied with the performance in the two areas was higher in 2009 than two years earlier and similar to their satisfaction with other health plans in the market.

Hawaii: New legislation established a State Facility Renovation Partnership Program in which the state may enter into P3s to modernize and repair aging state buildings. Under the program, the state's Department of Accounting and General Services can sell state buildings to private investors, who would finance renovations (or new facility construction) and lease the assets back to the state. The state would continue to own the land underneath the facility, and it would have the option to repurchase the facility back from the private partner.

Iowa: New legislation replaced the state's Department of Economic Development (DED) with a new public-private partnership intended to boost the state's economic development activities. The new Iowa Partnership for Economic Progress consists of a seven-member advisory board (Economic Progress Partnership); a new state-funded authority (Iowa Economic Development Authority) with its own politically appointed board; and a private, nonprofit economic development corporation (Iowa Innovation Corporation) responsible for raising private funds to help finance startup businesses.

Kentucky: Lawmakers approved a plan to privatize Medicaid services to help close a deficit in the state's Medicaid budget. The state awarded four contracts to managed care organizations to provide services to Medicaid recipients across Kentucky. Three of those contracts are with new vendors— CoventryCares of Kentucky, Kentucky Spirit Health Plan, and WellCare of Kentucky—and will serve more than 560,000 recipients. The state's existing annual contract with Passport, previously the state's only managed care provider, was renewed to provide services to 170,000 Medicaid recipients in Jefferson and fifteen nearby counties.

According to the administration, the new Medicaid managed care contracts will save $375 million in general fund spending and $1.3 billion across all funds over the course of the three-year contracts, allowing the state to fully balance the Medicaid budget in Fiscal Year 2012. The companies will create nearly 550 new jobs in Kentucky by January 1, 2012 to administer the managed care contracts, according to administration estimates. The administration received federal approval of the Medicaid changes, allowing the program to proceed to full implementation.

New Hampshire: New legislation was enacted that authorized a shift away from a Medicaid fee-for-service to a privatized managed care system. The New Hampshire Department of Health and Human Services issued a Request For Proposals from managed care organizations to cover administration of the state's Medicaid program.

New legislation was enacted authorizing auto dealers to act as agents of the state Division of Motor Vehicles for vehicle registrations and title applications. Previously, vehicles could only be registered at town or city halls. Under the new law, customers can electronically register their vehicles at the dealership when purchased.

New Mexico: New legislation was enacted giving in-state firms a preferential advantage over those based out of state in contracting for state construction projects. The new law treats bids by in-state firms as being 5 percent lower than actually submitted, creating a significant disadvantage for lower cost, out-of-state competitors.

North Carolina: The Program Evaluation Division began work on a study reviewing the operations of all state-owned attractions—including state parks, aquariums, historic areas, and the state-run zoo. The North Carolina Aquarium Society plans to take over operation of the state's three aquariums.

South Carolina: The administration received eight vendor responses to a Request For Information it issued soliciting proposals on how to privatize the only state-owned school bus fleet in the country.

Texas: Legislation enacted will expand the state's privatized Medicaid managed care program—currently utilized in several counties—statewide, a move designed to provide $467 million in budget savings. The bill also establishes a framework for the development of new health care collaboratives.

Utah: Newly enacted legislation requires the state's Department of Health, Department of Workforce Services and Privatization Policy Board to undertake a study of the state's Medicaid eligibility determination system to determine whether consolidation of the system or privatization would create greater efficiencies.

West Virginia: The five-year privatization of West Virginia's Workers' Compensation Commission was completed with a $19 million, one-year contract with Zurich

Insurance Co. to provide workers' compensation insurance to state agencies. The privatization was the result of a 2005 law transforming the Workers' Compensation Commission—the state-run monopoly insurer—into a private insurance carrier, BrickStreet Mutual Insurance Co. BrickStreet was given a temporary monopoly as it made the conversion to a private sector enterprise, and since 2008 has faced competition from other firms in the private sector market. Competition has driven down premium rates by nearly 52 percent since 2005. The initiative also dramatically reduced the outstanding unfunded liabilities of the old state-run system (from $3.2 billion to $1.9 billion in the first two years), the number of protested claims, and the amount of time required for a ruling on protested claims.

PART SIX

Appendices

Appendix 1: Preparing to Meet With Public Officials

Chart of Objectives and Preparations

Use the chart on the next several pages to prepare for calls on potential government customers. Virtually all of these tactics are designed to help gather information and intelligence because the bidder with the most information has the best chance of winning a bid and delivering a successful result.

Objective	Preparation
Have an appropriate message that outlines capabilities and services and customize it for each stakeholder you'll encounter.	Be prepared to leave a lasting impression of your core competencies with each stakeholder.
Identify decision-maker(s) and important stakeholders and get to know as much as possible about each.	Learn who is the individual with decision-making authority related to this opportunity? Who are other stakeholders and influencers?

Develop a one-page leave-behind customized for each meeting.	Deliver a clear and concise message specific to the meeting. Make sure the one-page document contains verbiage that describes your desired action and/or the value proposition of what you hope will be considered. Include your contact information. This document should convey the value proposition.
Know exactly what problem you are going to address. Focus your message so it is short, clear and easy to remember.	Numerous solutions or capabilities tend to confuse. Present a clear vision of what problems you can solve.
Identify the core business of the entity and tie your solution to a critical component of the mission or to enhancing the services the governmental entity provides.	Web sites are excellent sources of information as most clearly state the organization's core mission.
Know what differentiates you from competitors and be able to deliver this message clearly and persuasively.	You must be able to state your value proposition and then differentiate it from others. Find some area of excellence to discuss.
Know your company's history with other public sector entities in the area; be able to speak about your company's total presence in the region.	This enhances credibility and offers a sense of community and stability. It will also indicate experience and a positive track record.

Study the individuals who are influencers and analyze their concerns.	These are the people who will recommend for or against your solution or service. What matters to them is important.
Identify and prioritize who you need to develop a relationship with and why.	It is important to build and maximize a relationship. Purchasers buy from people they know and trust.
Know favored vendors of entity and consider the influence of each.	This is your competition and you need to know as much as possible. Are there any you can partner with? Can others provide you with information you need?
Analyze budget information.	What is being spent now or what is the budget for the project? Demonstrate that you are knowledgeable.
Know as much as possible about political groups that influence the potential customer. Gather information about these groups.	Are there multiple political entities involved? Oversight boards? Any information you can gather will be helpful and will provide you with a better understanding of the decision-maker's thought processes.
Understand the timing of political decision making and how it impacts the agency you are targeting.	When and how does funding occur? What is the process for political review of projects during selection process?
Understand funding cycle and processes. Consider where the decision-maker is in the cycle as you present your solution.	Annual or biennial budget process? When and how are requests submitted? Who is involved in the review? When is it approved?

Know regional/local political issues. Stay in touch locally and be aware of the many factions involved in current issues.	What are the major political problems on the radar that will influence all decisions?
Always be cordial, responsive and timely in your follow up to any agency official.	Listen to what is said to you... not all vendors do this. Provide requested information within days. Don't lose momentum.
Find ways to communicate regularly with governmental officials after you get to know them without always asking for something.	Decision makers want to see you as a professional acquaintance...not someone always seeking a favor. Lunch, ball games or calls to offer timely or valuable information are good.
Select or develop collateral material that uses public sector terminology, and is concise and on point. It should be customized for the meeting and person you are meeting with.	Avoid use of terms like profit margins, bottom line, revenue enhancement, etc. Make sure the collateral is exactly on point for what you intend to discuss.
Identify relevant references and be prepared to mention them in an appropriate way or include the data in your one-page leave behind.	Speak about references in similar organizations if possible. If not, describe why the reference is relevant.
Highlight problems that might trigger a need for your solution. Give them a vision of what problems you are capable of solving.	Helps your client know when to call on you for assistance.

Understand the current and relevant public sector environment. Trends that touch one agency usually spill over to other agencies in a locale.	Identifies you as a knowledgeable player in the marketplace.
Identify elected officials who may be connected to the problem you hope to solve.	Who has political oversight and what is important to them?
Be aware of federal/state/local legislation impacting the entity.	Is there a legal reason something must be done a certain way or in a certain time period? Are there mandates that the agency must satisfy?
Understand the fine line between what is acceptable and what is not when it comes to doing business with governmental officials.	Varies with each relationship and each governmental entity. It will be defined by the customer but vendors must be careful and know what is acceptable in each region.
Know and abide by state or local ethics laws.	Know the agency's policy and any overriding law. Never allow yourself to get into trouble or be penalized later because of questionable activities.
Find a way to mention something personal if appropriate.	Try to work some appropriate personal information into your conversations. Google usually provides information on most public servants.

Appendix 2: Bidders' Conferences Dos and Don'ts

When to Listen, When to Ask

1. Show up early and take the opportunity to mingle with other vendors, agency officials and the customer team.
2. Listen to what is being said around you. Often, good information is picked up in sidebar conversations. You can always attempt to verify it later.
3. Take all bidders' conferences seriously. This is a formal part of the procurement process and governmental entities usually ask their contracting and legal staffs to have someone there to oversee the process and answer questions.
4. Listen carefully to all answers to questions asked. Ask questions not answered, if appropriate. Your comments and questions should be carefully stated, but there are certain things you will need to know.
   - Are there areas of clarification that were not covered?
   - Do they anticipate any schedule changes?

- What will be the process for submitting future questions and getting access to answers?
- Is there a library of documentation related to the bid that will be available to potential bidders?

5. Make a list of all attendees and the companies they represent. Take good notes on who asks which questions. It is always good to ask for a copy of the sign-in sheet because you may later need contact information.

6. Examine other vendors in the audience for potential teaming partners as well as serious competitors.

7. Don't ask a question that will reveal anything to a competitor if you believe you are providing anything of importance. If you can gain enough information by not asking questions, it is best to remain silent.

8. If it is necessary to get some information relevant to your capture plan consider a way to submit it anonymously or find someone other than your team to ask the question. Note: To avoid asking a question that might tip your hand, some companies simply assume an answer they find favorable and proceed accordingly with their response. There is obvious danger related to this approach, but if you can't deal with an unfavorable answer, don't ask the question.

9. Don't ask a question about a potential evaluation concern unless you know the answer. Your objective is to find a way to ensure the question will be answered the way you want it to be. You can often use the Q&A period for asking the question in a more leading way to try and influence the answer.

10. Caution any outside experts who come for the conference about asking questions that might show he or she does not understand how things are done in the agency.

11. Do not ask questions to try and show them how smart you are.

12. Determine if the answers given at the bidders' conference are definitive and final responses. Many times, an official answer to the questions are the written responses posted on the procurement Web site, not the oral ramblings that occur during the actual conference.

Proposal Preparation Guidelines

SPI consultants have seen numerous large opportunities that were lost simply because some of these steps were not taken before the formal proposal was submitted. Here are the five critical components.

1. Rigid Process Requires A Checklist

- Public sector procurement usually involves very rigid requirements. Failure to comply, even with seemingly insignificant steps, can disqualify a proposal.

- Look to see if the procurement prohibits communication and/or lobbying. If so, follow the rules that limit your contact with agency employees once the RFP has been released. It is too late to secure insider information through FOIA once a bid has been released. Even if the agency decided to provide the information, most likely it would be released after the bid due date.

- Because governmental entities often receive dozens of proposals, it is common procedure to assign a procurement professional the task of checking all proposals to ensure strict compliance with every requirement of the bid document. Some agencies want to limit the number to be evaluated and this is a first step in that process. Therefore, the first step is to develop a detailed checklist of all requirements, assignment of responsibilities and critical timelines.

For example:

✔ There may be mandatory bidders' conferences that will require out-of-town travel.

✔ There is usually a deadline for question submission and a requirement that questions be in writing. It is important to factor such things into internal scheduling. Often, important questions don't arise until you draft the proposal, so if you start too late it is easy to miss the deadline for submitting questions.

✔ Some requirements, such as getting a tax ID in the jurisdiction, have prerequisite steps that take time to accomplish. The checklist (which for a complex proposal may need to be tracked in a Gantt chart) will ensure these time constraints can be met.

✔ It is very common to experience a hurried atmosphere as the deadline approaches and that makes it easy to overlook some seemingly bureaucratic details. For instance, you may be required to sign multiple forms in a specified ink color or may be required to sign amendments to the RFP to show you received them. The checklist will ensure nothing is missed.

✔ It is also common to run short on time as the deadline approaches. Pre-planning and strict adherence to a timeline with deadlines for all proposal team members is critically important. Proposals that arrive late will not be accepted. Never overlook the possibility of bad weather, illness on the part of an individual or any other situations that could cause problems, such as printing errors. Give yourself time to react if anything unexpected occurs.

- The Proposal Preparation Checklist lists some start-up actions and provides a useful format for you to use in creating a detailed checklist for a specific proposal.

2. Consider the Stakeholders

All good proposals are highly targeted to stakeholders. You must spend time identifying the audience. Proposals to public sector entities usually involve at least four groups of stakeholders and connecting with each is important.

- Procurement professionals: These are the people who perform the front-end work of ensuring strict compliance with all detailed requirements of a proposal.
- Program professionals: These are the people whose operations are directly impacted. They must feel comfortable that you are competent to do the job and reliable in terms of meeting deadlines. They (along with procurement professionals) will comprise the evaluation

team and make a recommendation to management. They are looking for low-risk, cost-efficient solutions.

- Final decision makers: Depending on the agency or entity, this may be a senior manager, the agency chief or a governing board. Usually, there will be several steps in the management chain between final decision makers and the program and procurement professionals. As strange as it sounds, the final decision makers may base their decision on a briefing summary and it is possible that these individuals will only see your executive summary, not your whole proposal. It is critically important that you make it easy for the program professionals to identify and be able to communicate your benefits to final decision makers. This may occur by offering your assistance if you are notified that staff will be recommending you to management or maybe by leaving a succinct one-page "leave-behind" at the oral presentations (if orals are part of the process). This audience is unlikely to delve into the technical details and more likely will be influenced by such matters as your reputation.

- The public: A major difference in public and private sector procurement is that most public sector documents are ultimately available to the public and losing competitors may ask to see your proposal based on the jurisdiction's freedom of information statutes. In light of this, some suggestions follow:

- ✔ Avoid informality in cover letters or anything else that could be used to suggest anything but an arm's length relationship.
- ✔ Same comment with regard to using phrases like "as we discussed."
- ✔ Clearly indicate any material that is a trade secret. The RFP may include instructions for specifying such information. You will not make the final decision on what is public information; however, designating specific information as trade secret or proprietary will probably result in the government's lawyers talking to your lawyers before a decision is made. It may be necessary to seek the assistance of your company's lawyers to advise you on what materials can be considered confidential.

3. Maximizing Your Proposal Team

For large proposals, a proposal-writing team will often be formed and individuals will be tasked to draft various sections. All members of the team should read these tips before beginning the proposal-writing process. Below are suggestions for structuring and tasking the team:

- Recognizing that styles differ, it is important that a single skilled writer has responsibility for the final draft. Depending on the complexity, there may need to be many people producing earlier drafts of specific sections, but you risk having the proposal sound disjointed or uncoordinated if one person isn't given final editing authority.

- It will save a lot of time for the team leader to issue a list of acceptable acronyms and the way to refer to the agency to which the bid is submitted. For example, if the bid is being submitted to the Wyoming Procurement Commission, one team member may refer to them as "the state," another calls them "the commission," while a third calls them "WPC." The decision on which label to use should consider local political sensitivities. For instance, in multiple agency procurements or in situations where a central procurement agency is buying on behalf of an end-user agency, in some contexts it may be preferable to refer to "the state" in order to avoid inadvertently referring to the wrong agency or referring to a single agency to the perceived exclusion of another.
- Assign a key team member to attend the bidders' conference(s) so that you have first-hand information. Answers to questions submitted are very important. Identifying potential competitors is also extremely important. Often it is also possible to get a better understanding and a "feel" for what the governmental entity is seeking if someone is physically present. Also, government procurement people are definitely aware of which vendors attend such meetings.
- Plan ahead as to who will participate in oral

presentations. Select good communicators and decide how each person will participate in the proposal-drafting process. Decisions will have to be made about what points to emphasize, what references to give and what examples to include in the proposal. It is important that those who will have to "defend" or explain the proposal are very comfortable with the approach taken in the written document.

- All proposals must have a reading team comprised of more than one final proofreader. Readers should read the final document for clarity, simplicity, correctness and a tone that depicts a commitment to customer satisfaction. All readers should try to read the document from a public sector perspective. Readers should also look for wording that offers evaluators a comfort zone in the areas of credibility, experience and cost justification. Assign someone to cross-check requirements with your responses. There should be as many local connections as possible and wording that is supportive of the governmental entity and validates the reason for change or outsourcing.

4. Proposal Contents

- Most RFPs have a required format for submitting responses. Follow it! If only general bid format instructions are provided, organize your bid so that specifications are clearly linked to responses. Respond to every specification. Some purchasers will comb through all bids and may eliminate any that don't respond to each question or to the specified format. Other bid specs may allow the government to waive minor errors and omissions, but you should not risk it. Every blank must be filled in and every question must be answered. There are simply no exceptions.

- Make the proposal easy to read. Break up sections with bullet points if necessary. Consider the person who must plow through dozens of proposals and make yours memorable.

- An RFP response is your company's resume—a presentation of the facts—as well as an opportunity to "sell" yourself. Differentiate your response as much as possible. Spend some time on developing a creative approach to the final product. Try to sell the fact that your solution and your reputation are "low risk."

- Responses to requirements should be fact- or process-oriented. Don't respond with "We understand and agree." Instead, explain in business process terms exactly how you will meet the requirement.

- In your enthusiasm to explain how your product or service may improve the current environment, be careful not to disparage the current system. It may have been designed by a program professional who will be serving on the evaluation team.

- Separate and clearly label alternative proposals to avoid confusion about responsiveness to the actual specs.
- Price only those items required by the specifications. Optional features should be priced separately or left subject to negotiation. Remember the importance of being a low-cost option. You don't always have to be the lowest in cost, but you must not be much higher.
- Although best value is usually the ultimate selection criteria, budget ceilings may eliminate a bid that is high value but priced higher than other bidders.
- The Executive Summary should be far more than an abstract that precedes the rest of the proposal; it's your unique opportunity to convince the reader that your proposal provides the best value. A great deal of attention must be focused on this part of the proposal. Most likely, everyone involved in the procurement will read this section. Many of the evaluators read only the Executive Summary and one small piece of the proposal. Further, Executive Summaries should be supportive of the agency, the reason for the procurement and offer a listing of benefits that are being offered through the proposed solution. The more technical your proposal, the more critical the Executive Summary is likely to be.
- Verify the contact information of any

references. Most evaluation teams will make calls and wrong phone numbers are frustrating. Since contact information often changes, take the time to verify every piece of information you provide.

- Many firms spend all their time working on price and overlook the writing process. Other firms may use "canned proposal parts" and simply cut and paste. Both approaches make it easy to produce an unacceptable proposal. If a firm cuts and pastes from old proposal documents, it is very easy to use a wrong name, state or acronym in the document. When such mistakes are made, it makes evaluators very uneasy about your delivery of services. This can be a costly mistake and it usually happens when timelines begin to run short or when seasoned readers are not reviewing the final product.
- Localize proposals as much as possible. Localizing can be done by pointing out individuals within the state or local government who will be involved. It could also be done by pointing to the company's presence in the state (i.e., the number of employees) or other customers located in the state. Localizing can also be done by pointing to experience with other governmental agencies in the same category. If necessary, it can even be accomplished by listing other current customers with similar problems or issues.
- Carefully evaluate how doing work offshore

will be viewed by the customer. Some states are very critical of this approach even when the result is a cost savings. Never suggest sending customer data offshore unless the customer has indicated that this would be agreeable. Be aware that this practice is often a political issue that gets bad publicity.

- Many RFPs suggest disadvantaged businesses or minority subcontractor participation. Questions should always be directed to the agency concerning this issue. Usually there are strict guidelines that must be followed to ensure that prime contractors make a "good faith effort" to secure minority subcontractors. Many proposals have been disqualified simply because a proposal did not have anything that convincingly pointed to a good faith effort to secure minority partners.

- Public sector contracts often contain terms that are not common in commercial contracts. Consequently, there may be unfamiliar terms that you should have reviewed by your attorneys or contract professionals. For example, agencies may consider your bid (and any resulting work product) to be a public sector document, so your attorney may want to consider how best to protect any proprietary information. Public sector contracts also frequently decline to limit consequential damages and require liquidated damages, indemnities, bonding and other terms that are less often

found in private sector contracts. Avoid
taking exceptions to terms and conditions in
your bid whenever possible. Most issues can
be dealt with during contract negotiations.
If you object to terms and conditions
early in the process, you may never get
an opportunity to get issues clarified or
negotiated.

5. Submitting the Proposal

Submitting the proposal may seem simple, but again recall that public sector procurement is subject to rigid processes. A recent Georgia case makes the point. A vendor submitted proposal information by email (which was allowed by the procedures), but the email was stopped by the procurement officer's spam filter. The proposal was discovered later but the discovery came after the deadline and by then the vendor had already been disqualified. The message is clear. No proposal should be considered submitted until you have some type of legal verification that the agency or governmental entity has received and accepted it in a timely manner.

Final Tip

Read this checklist before starting the proposal process. Read it again after you have prepared the final document.